ORDE
WINGATE

LEADERSHIP ■ STRATEGY ■ CONFLICT

JON DIAMOND ■ ILLUSTRATED BY PETER DENNIS

First published in 2012 by Osprey Publishing
Midland House, West Way, Botley, Oxford OX2 0PH, UK
44-02 23rd St, Suite 219, Long Island City, NY 11101, USA
E-mail: info@ospreypublishing.com
© 2012 Osprey Publishing Limited

OSPREY PUBLISHING IS PART OF THE OSPREY GROUP

Print ISBN: 978 1 84908 323 2
PDF e-book ISBN: 978 1 84908 324 9
EPUB e-book ISBN: 978 1 78200 300 7

Editorial by Ilios Publishing Ltd, Oxford, UK (www.iliospublishing.com)
Cartography: Mapping Specialists Ltd.
Design: The Black Spot
Index by Mark Swift
Originated by PDQ Digita; Media Solutions Ltd., UK
Printed in China through Worldprint

12 13 14 15 16   10 9 8 7 6 5 4 3 2 1

A CIP catalogue record for this book is available from the British Library.

For a catalogue of all books published by Osprey Military and Aviation please contact:

www.ospreypublishing.com

Imperial War Museum Collections

The photographs in this book come from the Imperial War Museum's huge collections, which cover all aspects of conflict involving Britain and the Commonwealth since the start of the 20th century. These rich resources are available online to search, browse and buy at www.iwmcollections.org.uk. In addition to collections online, you can visit the visitor rooms where you can explore over 8 million photographs, thousands of hours of moving images, the largest sound archive of its kind in the world, thousands of diaries and letters written by people in wartime and a huge reference library. To make an appointment, call (020) 7416 5320, or e-mail mail@iwm.org.uk.

www.iwm.org.uk

Artist's note

Readers may care to note that the original paintings from which the colour plates in this book were prepared are available for private sale. All reproduction copyright whatsoever is retained by the Publishers. All enquiries should be addressed to:

Peter Dennis, Fieldhead, The Park, Mansfield, Notts, NG18 2AT
Email: magieh@ntlworld.com

The Publishers regret that they can enter into no correspondence upon this matter.

Front-cover image: Cody Images

The Woodland Trust
Osprey Publishing are supporting the Woodland Trust, the UK's leading woodland conservation charity, by funding the dedication of trees. To celebrate the Queen's Diamond Jubilee we are proud to support the Woodland Trust's Jubilee Woods Project.

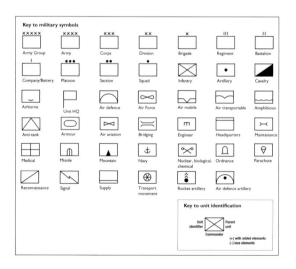

CONTENTS

INTRODUCTION

Major-General Orde Charles Wingate, DSO (1903–44) was one of the more enigmatic commanders of World War II. His military career has filled many books, focusing on his personality and command dynamics as it relates to the development of his strategic ideas on guerrilla warfare and the tactical use of long-range penetration (LRP). Wingate's memory is revered in many places, notably Israel, where he is referred to as *Hayedid*, 'the Friend'. Controversies still swirl about his reputation almost 70 years after his death in an aeroplane crash in the jungles of Burma.

A regular British Army officer during the interwar period plodded through the peacetime promotion system, while attending numerous staff college courses and seeing action only on Salisbury Plain. In contrast, Wingate's career was sequentially layered with different assignments built on leading small, behind-the-lines units, first against Britain's enemies in the colonies and mandates of the empire. Later, during World War II, he led attacks in East Africa and Burma, demonstrating imaginative leadership and courage. These experiences formed Wingate's doctrine, which was enacted often with the support of powerful military and political patrons.

The word 'guerrilla', or irregular soldier, is derived from the Spanish for war, *guerra*. During the Peninsular War, Spanish guerrillas supported Wellington by cutting French lines of communications, principally through ambush, forcing Napoleon's marshals to divert troops simply to protect them. Wingate's view of guerrilla or irregular warfare evolved from his first-hand experiences as a junior officer in the Sudan Defence Force, combating local brigands (*shiftas*), to his creation of an anti-insurgency force, the Special Night Squads, which ambushed Arab gangs sabotaging the Iraqi oil pipeline during the Arab Revolt of 1936–38 in Palestine. In Ethiopia in 1941 he helped raise and field a British-led guerrilla or 'Patriot' insurrection, Gideon Force, to oust the Italians from the Gojjam Province of Ethiopia, ultimately contributing to the Italian defeat and the restoration of Emperor Haile Selassie's throne.

Each command became serially larger until his most famous, when he led the Chindit organization in Burma, where he was able to give free rein to his ideas of long-range penetration behind enemy lines, with Operation *Longcloth* in 1943 and then as Special Force or 3rd (Indian) Division for Operation *Thursday* in 1944. Bernard Fergusson, who commanded Column 5 in Operation *Longcloth* and a brigade in Operation *Thursday* believed that Wingate's ideas clashed with Army dogma: 'On the whole [Wingate] failed to convert current military thought to his belief in deep penetration. He certainly convinced his lieutenants'. Nonetheless, Wingate's rigorous training and operational standards for these formations have served as models for post-war elite anti-terrorist and special operation troops.

The spectrum of opinion about Wingate's military principles and ideas is quite wide. Exemplifying this is a statement from Churchill's eulogy of Wingate in the House of Commons on 22 August 1944: 'There was a man of genius, who might well have become also a man of destiny'. Alternatively, Major-General Julian Thompson wrote,

Wingate and his immediate commander, Gen. William Slim, at Lalaghat airfield in Assam preceding the glider airlift of Calvert's 77th Indian Brigade on 5 March 1944, the start of Operation *Thursday*. (IWM, HU 70592)

Much of what he preached was strategically, operationally, and tactically flawed, and some of it was downright nonsense.... He was a man of many moods and fiery temperament. He could be outrageously offensive – especially to his seniors and their staffs. The unswerving loyalty he demanded from his subordinates he conspicuously withheld from his superiors, thinking nothing of going over their heads, lying, plotting, and lobbying to get his own way. He was either hated or loved; there was no middle ground with Wingate.

According to Philip Warner, 'it is not unusual for unorthodox and daring wartime commanders to be labelled "mad" by their critics. General Wolfe, the conqueror of Quebec, and thus, Canada, is a case in point. A contemporary said: "General Wolfe is mad". George III, retorted: "Mad is he. I wish he would bite some of my other generals".' To his critics, Wingate was a charlatan who owed his triumphs to high-ranking patrons. With unorthodox opinions on many matters, he actively sought argument, especially with senior officers, and often attacked them directly in his official memoranda with insulting language.

His most vocal critic, Major-General S. Woodburn Kirby, lead author of the *Official History of the War against Japan*, stated, 'Just as timing played so great a part in his rise to prominence, so the moment of his death may have been propitious for him. He was killed at the height of his career and was not called upon to face the inevitable fact that his dreams and ambitions could never have been realized'. Kirby further railed,

The way in which his ideas on the use of long-range penetration forces grew in Wingate's fertile imagination would form an interesting psychological study. From his early conception of lightly armed troops penetrating behind the enemy lines and attacking communications as part of a larger operation by conventional forces, the operations of Special Force clearly became in his mind the only means by which northern Burma could be dominated. Subsequently, much increased in numbers, the force would become the spearhead of a victorious advance through southern Burma, Siam and Indo-China to win the war against Japan.

In Kirby's verdict, Wingate was at best a drain on scarce military assets in Burma, whose work was based on ill-formed ideas under the military patronage of Wavell and Mountbatten and the political support of Leo Amery and Churchill.

Another posthumous critic of Wingate was Fourteenth Army Commander, Field Marshal Viscount Slim who wrote in his post-war memoirs, 'When he [Wingate] found argument failed, he turned to sterner measures. Such had been his romantic success with the Prime Minister that he claimed the right to send him messages direct, with his views and recommendations, irrespective of whether Admiral Mountbatten or any other superior commander agreed with them or not'. Slim also believed that elite units siphoned regular troops from the larger forces that could be deployed to beat Japan's major units in battle, such as occurred at Imphal. Intriguingly, Slim praised the Chindit leader immediately after his death, specifically eulogizing him for his genius.

THE EARLY YEARS

Wingate was born on 26 February 1903 in Naini Tal in India. Wingate's ancestors apparently arrived in England during the Norman Conquest and the family's French name was originally Winguet. Orde Wingate's branch of the family settled in Scotland and produced financially successful merchants in Glasgow. Wingate's father, George, was born in 1852 and entered the British Army in 1871. Having served with the Green Howards, he transferred to the Indian Army and amidst the religious fervour of India he had a religious experience that compelled him to join the Plymouth Brethren sect. While on leave in England, George Wingate fell in love at first sight with Ethel Orde-Browne, then only 12 years old, who was also a young member of the Plymouth Brethren. Twenty years passed until then Colonel George Wingate was able to marry Ethel at Woolwich in September 1899. Coincidentally, years later, his son Orde was similarly smitten when he first met his future wife, Lorna, in 1933 when she was only 16.

A generation before, it was Ethel's father, Charles Orde-Browne, who while serving as an artillery officer in the Crimea, also converted to the Plymouth Brethren sect from the Church of England amid the horrors of war. In north Woolwich, Charles Orde-Browne, Wingate's maternal grandfather, served as an unordained minister, but in order to generate an income, he lectured on mathematics at the Royal Military Academy, Woolwich. Thus, through Orde's mother came Charles' restless intellectual curiosity and an interest in a diverse set of subjects from philosophy to poetry to music.

After Colonel Wingate retired from the Army at age 52, the family moved back from India to Sussex. He continued to address the Brethren congregation every Sunday and his fellow members sometimes said, 'The Colonel has a gift for the ministry'.

Young Orde Wingate 'showed no extraordinary proficiency, no unusual alertness of mind, no sign of exceptional gifts'. Even though he was rigorously home-schooled by his mother and tutors, young 'Ordey... remained perversely slow at his books'. Throughout his childhood, like his siblings, Wingate was insulated from other children his age. This ended, when at the age of 13, Orde was sent to a private school called Hill Side. His contemporaries had very few flattering memories of young Wingate, and what was recorded was quite derogatory: 'a small uncommunicative untidy little scalliwag with a stooping gait'; 'a little rat-like fellow'; 'Stinker'; 'you could see even then he had a will'. According to a classmate, with whom Wingate shared mutual interests, Jossleyn Hennessy, 'Wingate presented himself to the school as being dour, unsociable, even unlikable'.

In September 1916, Orde Wingate started at Charterhouse. Again, he was a 'day boy' as opposed to a boarder at the school and as such, Wingate was considered 'to be if not unusual then at least different because they could not participate fully in the school's life'. His attire differed in some respects from the other boys at Charterhouse. His uniform was made of poorer quality material and he wore boots rather than shoes. Although on the surface, this may appear trivial, it did engender a sense of deprivation as the dress code was a matter of some importance at the school. Wingate's strict adherence to the Plymouth Brethren's credo was also at odds with the Anglican majority at Charterhouse. Wingate's exclusion from mainstream school life placed him in the same predicament as the Jewish boys who attended Charterhouse in relatively large numbers. During his four-year attendance at Charterhouse, Wingate 'won no prize and distinguished himself in no branch of study or athletics'. Wingate 'was wretchedly unhappy.... He felt persecuted.... There is no evidence that in fact he was'. However, he despised organized sports at Charterhouse and refused to participate in house or school games, but apparently developed into a good marksman with the rifle.

In November 1920, at the age of 17, Wingate passed his examination for the Royal Military Academy, Woolwich and entered that august institution for 'gunners and engineers' on 3 February 1921. With his family's military tradition behind him, Wingate believed that military force would still be required in the future, despite the peace initiatives after 1918, and his decision to become a soldier had a sound, pragmatic basis. As for Woolwich, Wingate was also keenly aware one would require a substantial private income as an officer in a cavalry or infantry regiment, and chose to become either an engineer or artillery officer since both corps expected their officers to subsist on their military salary alone. In addition, the fees at Woolwich were considerably less than those at Sandhurst. Wingate passed into Woolwich 63rd out of 69 entrants. Those who achieved higher marks on the examination usually opted for the Royal Engineers or the Royal Field Artillery, while those, like Wingate, with lower marks were allotted to the Royal Garrison Artillery.

MILITARY LIFE

Royal Military Academy, Woolwich 1921–23

At Woolwich, Wingate studied subjects such as tactics, military law, cartography, close-order drill, and riding – at which Wingate excelled. Being untidy, he was constantly teased by his fellow cadets. He responded by ignoring 'ludicrous' rules, which led to the ultimate punishment of running naked through a group of cadets armed with swagger sticks and towels, ending with a violent immersion into a water tank. Legend has it that Wingate walked through them slowly, glaring at his tormentors so that few dared to strike him and, in the end, he dove into the water tank gaining the admiration of many of the harassing cadets. In July 1923, Wingate passed out 59th out of 70, relegating him to the Royal Garrison Artillery with the 18th Medium Battery on Salisbury Plain.

Wingate (wearing civilian clothing) stands with SNS troops wearing their pre-war denim fatigues with serge field service caps in Palestine, 1938. (Author's collection)

The interwar British Army had been pared down; promotion was slow and there was limited active service abroad. For career advancement, Orde began a correspondence in 1924 with his father's cousin, Sir Reginald Wingate ('Cousin Rex') for professional guidance. Cousin Rex had been Kitchener's Director of Military Intelligence during the Sudan Campaign and later served as the Governor-General of the Sudan, *Sirdar* or Commander-in-Chief of the Egyptian Army and British High Commissioner in Cairo.

Wingate was promoted to full lieutenant in 1925 and with Cousin Rex's encouragement, enrolled at the University of London as an Arabic language student in 1926, to qualify as an interpreter for a Middle East posting, hoping that this was a route to active service abroad. Later that year, Wingate wrote *Strategy in Three Campaigns*, examining the Russo-Japanese War, the Schlieffen Plan, and Allenby's Palestine victory, the last of which he praised for its skilful tactics and fleetness of

Wingate's area of operations in the Sudan

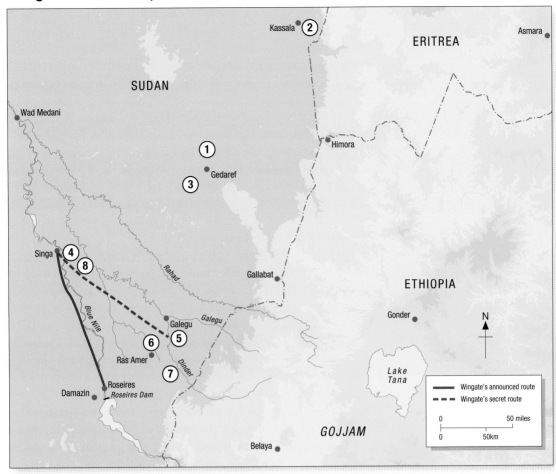

1. 1924: Sudan Defence Force (SDF) formed and its East Arab Corps (EAC) headquartered at Gedaref in Kassala Province with major stations at Kassala, Singa, Roseires and Gallabat.
2. March 1930: Wingate's No. 3 *Idara* is based at Kassala near the border with Eritrea.
3. Early 1931: Wingate ordered to lead a patrol into the Dinder and Gallegu country in pursuit of Ethiopian poachers (*shifta*), who had been kidnapping Sudanese from border tribes and killing animals in the game reserves.
4. 11 April 1931: Wingate leads two sections of No. 3 *Idara* out of Singa announcing that his destination was the town of Roseires to the south.
5. 12–18 April 1931: In order to get between the gangs and their sanctuary and take them by surprise Wingate secretly changes course eastwards to the river Dinder.
6. 19 April 1931: two poachers captured and disclose whereabouts of the main *shifta* party. Wingate surrounds the poacher gang near Ras Amer and a firefight ensues.
7. 21 April 1931: Wingate's patrol traps another band of 11 poachers killing one and arresting the remainder. Wingate pursues other *shifta* but the hard terrain, low ammunition and tired mounts end the chase.
8. 26 April 1931: Convinced that the poaching gang has dispersed, the patrol returns to Singa.

mobility to overcome an opponent's numerical advantage. Cousin Rex also encouraged Wingate to continue his Arabic studies in the Sudan and to apply to the Sudan Defence Force (SDF) for a posting. The former governor-general wrote a letter of introduction to the SDF's commander, helping to oil the wheels of advancement for Orde. This was the first example of Wingate's talent for acquiring powerful patrons to whom he could appeal outside the formal chain of command.

Sudan Defence Force

Wingate served with the SDF's East Arab Corps (EAC) from 1928 to 1933. Initially a subaltern, in March 1930 Wingate became *Bimbashi* (acting major) of No. 3 *Idara (*Infantry Company), an independent command of 375 men. The EAC was headquartered in Gedaref, in Kassala Province with Wingate's *Idara* stationed in Kassala near the Eritrean border. This isolated backwater allowed Wingate to demonstrate command initiative and develop military principles about small groups of soldiers surviving in a desolate, inhospitable environment, which would have been almost impossible for his rank in the regular British Army. Training, fitness, and field craft became his credos, which would enable his troops to remain active far from their garrison beyond the lines of communication. Marching his *Idara* 500 miles into remote areas of eastern Sudan, Wingate experimented with ground-to-air control by working with RAF Squadron 47 (B), and laid the foundations of this emerging tactic for future commands.

In early 1931, Wingate led a patrol against Ethiopian poachers and slave-traders (*shifta*), in the Dinder and Gallegu river border country of eastern Sudan. The SDF maintained border security via infantry or police patrols, which were intended to track down the gangs and arrest or destroy them. From 11 to 26 April, Wingate's Dinder Patrol, made up of two sections of his *Idara* managed to surprise the gangs and prevent their escape to a border sanctuary. He later employed a similar tactic in Palestine. On 11 April, Wingate left Singa, on the Blue Nile, letting it be known that he was heading due south to Roseires. He soon deviated east to the Dinder River region to deceive any spies who might be monitoring his route. This mode of deception would be standard Wingate fare for the rest of his career. In pursuit of the poachers, Wingate was impressed by their ability to scatter and re-form under the threat of attack, which influenced his tactics of dispersal and rendezvous that he employed years later with the Chindits in Burma. Over the next four days, Wingate had three separate violent encounters with the *shifta,* killing a handful and arresting several others. Since Wingate knew that the *shifta* could elude his patrol in the Dinder's brush if alerted, he devised tactics that depended on deception, surprise and selection of the best areas for ambushes. Throughout his career, Wingate would stress all of these tactical points.

During the last months of his posting in Sudan, Wingate spent six weeks of leave exploring Libya's Sea of Sand in search of the lost oasis of Zerzura. His accounts were published in the *Geographical Magazine* the following April. He never found Zerzura and his small expedition accomplished little, other than to collect specimens and discover that the oasis 'did not lie on the Kufra road'. However, the trek emboldened Wingate further and convinced him that he could lead men and survive in an unforgiving environment.

After his Sudanese service, Wingate was posted to the 9th Field Brigade stationed in Wiltshire. In 1935, Wingate was promoted to captain and started studying for the Staff College. Coupled with his memories of deprivation in the desert and mourning a sister's sudden death, Wingate suffered from unforeseen bouts of depression with his only remedy being found in his work. These bouts were contemporaneous with a broken engagement and then, his courtship with the much younger Lorna Paterson. The two were married on 24 January 1935 in a quiet family ceremony.

In the autumn of 1935, Wingate was posted to Sheffield as the adjutant to a Territorial Army formation, the 71st (West Riding) Field Brigade, Royal Artillery, again giving him a good deal of responsibility for his rank. After initially failing the written examination for the Staff College in February 1936, he passed on his second try four months later. However, even with the support of 'Cousin Rex', Wingate was not nominated for the Staff College. Taking matters into his own hands, Wingate approached the new Chief of the Imperial General Staff (CIGS), General Sir Cyril Deverell, when he came to inspect the Territorials' manoeuvres. He asked whether his Zerzura essay had been taken into account on his application to the staff college. Wingate regarded his own forward manner as merely a subordinate's initiative, rather than self-promotion and Deverell promised to look into the matter.

SNS troops wearing varied uniforms including Australian felt hat, field service cap and dress service cap. Articles of clothing include khaki drill, denim fatigues and pullover sweater. (Author's collection)

Palestine

Although Deverell could not place Wingate at either of the staff colleges, the CIGS did arrange for a posting as an intelligence officer (GSO I) with the 5th Division in Palestine on 7 September 1936. This was not a tranquil assignment, since an Arab revolt, starting with a general strike in April 1936, had culminated in clashes between Jews and Arabs along with acts of sabotage by Arab insurgents. The British 5th and 8th Divisions had been sent into Palestine to restore order.

Soon after his arrival, Wingate veered from the Army's pro-Arab stance and developed pro-Zionist sentiments. Nurtured with Old Testament biblical history and now educating himself about Palestine and its peoples, under the guise of intelligence gathering, he took on the 'plight of the Jews' and befriended many influential Zionists. Wingate believed that a Jewish homeland could become a better bastion for Britain's interests in the Middle East than anything that competing Arab groups could offer. He also regarded the establishment of a Jewish homeland as the fulfilment of religious prophecy and allied himself absolutely with Zionist leaders. After becoming intelligence officer at Corps HQ, Wingate stated, 'I tell you that the Jews will provide a soldiery better than ours. We have only to train it. They will equip it'. His fellow officer and colleague, Lieutenant Anthony Simonds of the Royal Berkshire Regiment also offered his services to this cause.

After a peaceful interlude, on 27 September 1937, the Arab Revolt was rekindled when the acting District Commissioner for Galilee was murdered in Nazareth. General Archibald Wavell, now General Officer Commanding (GOC), Palestine, issued warrants for the arrest of Higher Arab Committee members, and the Grand Mufti of Jerusalem went into hiding. However, within weeks the Arab insurrection literally blazed anew as saboteurs regularly set the Iraq Petroleum Company's pipeline to Haifa on fire. Now with fewer British regulars, Wavell began to use the Jewish Supernumerary Police (JSP), to fight the Arab insurgents. Wingate went so far as to back the *Haganah*, the illegal Jewish defence force, which in his mind was a 'priceless asset in the war against Arab terrorism'. Wingate advocated the formation of small units of soldiers to be used offensively against the Arab insurgents in his papers, *A Desert Force for Palestine* (1938) and *Palestine in Imperial Strategy* (1939), the latter written for a future CIGS, General Sir Edmund Ironside. These ideas gave rise to the creation of the Special Night Squads (SNS), which were composed of Jewish paramilitary volunteers reinforced by small numbers of British troops and led by British officers. Brigadier John Evetts, 16th Brigade commander in Haifa, who had fought both the Arab gangs and the North-west Frontier's militant tribesmen, was enthused with Wingate's idea.

With only two infantry brigades (rather than the 5th and 8th Divisions) to enforce order, Wavell relied on his own unorthodoxy to overcome the numerical odds. The British Army response – occupying Arab villages and using large units to patrol the surrounding countryside – was ineffective. Wavell needed new tactics, and Wingate presented it to him as the SNS force. Wavell gave his consent to form such units and later wrote, 'When I commanded in Palestine in 1937–1938, I had on my staff two officers in whom I recognized an original, unorthodox outlook on soldiering.... One was Orde Wingate'. Wavell added, 'I carried away in the corner of my mind an impression of a notable character who might be valuable as a leader of unorthodox enterprise in war, if I should ever have need of one'. On Wavell's orders, Wingate first visited Jewish settlements in Galilee in February 1938 to

Special Night Squad (SNS) operation north of Ein Harod, 11 June 1938

The oil pipeline running through Galilee was Wingate's main responsibility. On 11 June two mixed British/Jewish SNS patrols, each of 20 men with one British officer, left Ein Harod, their HQ village after dark for the pipeline to the north. The SNS were lightly armed with rifles, bayonets, ammunition bandoliers, and hand grenades. Wingate's preferred method of attacking the Arab gangs was close combat using grenades and bayonets. At Danna, a small hamlet east of Afula, the SNS spotted an Arab raiding party about 300 yards away setting fire to the pipeline. There was a loud explosion as the pipeline was punctured and escaping oil ignited. The SNS grenade-throwers ran forward and threw their bombs under covering fire from both patrols, while others chased the gang towards Danna. The patrols ultimately surrounded the Arab gang and found two dead and three wounded raiders. Six others were captured. For days following this raid, there was no further sabotage on the pipeline.

discover the routes by which the Arab insurgents were entering Palestine from Syria and Lebanon. Wingate scouted for suitable areas for small-unit mobile ambushes, since he believed that both static defences and truck-borne patrols were useless in preventing Arab gang attacks.

Lieutenant-General Sir Robert Haining, a gunner with considerable experience in intelligence, replaced Wavell in April 1938. He made British military superiority at night mandatory and in May 1938 authorized Evetts and Wingate to train JSP to patrol the pipeline and to carry out nighttime 'ambush work' in the 16th Brigade area. Wingate's new commander later wrote,

SNS members from the 1st Bn., Manchester Regt., commanding officer Lt. King-Clarke, in Palestine, 1938. (IWM, HU 37960)

> I cannot speak too highly... of the Special Night Squads... organized and trained by Captain OC WINGATE, Royal Artillery, from my Staff, who has shown great resource, enterprise and courage in leading and controlling their activities. These Squads have been supplemented by Jewish supernumeraries who have done excellent work in combination with the British personnel. The story of the inception and gradual development of this form of activity, and its successful results, provide a great tribute to the initiative and ingenuity of all concerned.

In May 1938, Wingate established his HQ at Ein Harod in north-eastern Palestine near both Trans-Jordan and Lebanon's borders, while also covering his primary responsibility, the oil pipeline. His second-in-command was Lieutenant Humphrey Bredin of the Royal Ulster Rifles, while Lieutenant Robert 'Rex' King-Clark of the Manchester Regiment was another of Wingate's officers. Wingate organized each British component of the SNS with ten enlisted men volunteers, an NCO and an officer, quartering them only in Jewish settlements to maintain security. In June 1938, an Army Order was issued allowing JSP throughout Palestine to patrol and carry out ambushes outside their settlements. Men from the JSP (*Noters*) and *Haganah* became the Jewish volunteers for the SNS. On 5 June 1938, Wingate wrote an *Appreciation* on

> The possibilities of night movements by armed forces of the Crown with the object of putting an end to terrorism in Northern Palestine.... Surprise has always been inflicted by the gangs, not by our forces... only one way... to persuade the gangs that, in their predatory raids, there is every chance of their running into a government gang, which is determined to destroy them, not by an exchange of shots at a distance, but by bodily assault with bayonet and bomb... for which they are totally unfitted.

On its first nocturnal ambush, on 3 June 1938, Wingate led an SNS patrol, scattering some pipeline saboteurs and wounding two. On 11–12 June, Wingate took three SNS groups to Jurdieh, after he initially marched through Lebanon to attack the village from the rear, in order to 'destroy' the Arab gang there. Two Arab saboteurs were killed, and attacks on the pipeline ceased for over a week. On 10/11 July Dabburiya was attacked by three SNS teams, fulfilling Wingate's wish to intimidate his enemy. Ten terrorists were killed outright, with four more bodies recovered the following morning. For this, Wingate received the Distinguished Service Order (DSO), while the pipeline had been breached only three times in the previous eight weeks. In early September, at Beit Lidd, on a route in which Arab insurgents crossed from Galilee into Samaria, five SNS groups surrounded 40 sleeping terrorists prior to their pipeline raid. Wingate's troops killed 14 and captured two of them.

Wingate's controversial reprisal attacks to suppress the pipeline sabotage began in mid-September, just a few hours after the head of Ein Harod was killed by a mine. Wingate raided the nearby Arab village of Beisan, issuing orders to round up all suspected rebels and shoot those trying to escape. At least two insurgents were killed. On 23 September another large-scale raid was mounted on Danna, where two high-ranking insurgents had returned from Syria and were reassembling a gang there. Twelve terrorists and the gang's leader were killed. A large operation was launched on 2 October 1938 to avenge the slaughter of Jewish children and adults at Tiberias. Wingate quickly deployed two SNS patrols that were in the vicinity and ambushed the Arab gang on its way out of Tiberias, killing at least 14 of them. The SNS was the only British unit to engage the Arab forces of Tiberias that night. On the next day, the SNS caught the remainder of the gang

General Sir Archibald Wavell, one of Wingate's principal patrons and commanders in Palestine, at his desk in Cairo as C-in-C, Middle East, 1939. Wavell served under Allenby in Palestine in 1917 and had a penchant for using unorthodoxy to overcome numerical inferiority in combat. (IWM, E 450)

Wingate's area of operations in Palestine

1. 1936–38: Arab rebels regularly sabotage the IPC pipeline across northern Palestine.
2. February 1938: Wingate visits Jewish settlements in Galilee to discover terrorist gang routes into Palestine from Syria and Lebanon.
3. May 1938: Wingate establishes his SNS HQ at Ein Harod in the Plain of Esdraelon with specific responsibility for protecting the oil pipeline.
4. 3 June 1938: SNS sees its first skirmish when a Wingate-led patrol ambushes and scatters Arab saboteurs on the pipeline, wounding two gang members.
5. 11 June 1938: Two patrols corner an Arab gang in the village of Danna, east of Afula, and in the raid kill two and capture six insurgents.
6. 17 June 1938: Wingate leads three SNS on an assault on the village of Jurdeih on the Palestine–Lebanon border and take the raiding force through Lebanon to ambush the Arab gang from the rear. Two insurgents are killed.
7. 5 July 1938: Lt. Bredin leads a patrol of four Royal Ulster Rifles and five Jewish SNS men. They are attacked by over a hundred Arab rebels near Danna. Bredin divides his force and initiates a pincer movement putting the Arab gang to flight.
8. 10/11 July 1938: three SNS raid Dabburiya in which ten terrorists are killed with four more bodies being recovered the next day. Wingate receives the DSO for this action in which he escalates the attack to terrorist bases as an act of intimidation. He is also wounded in the right arm and both legs by 'friendly fire'.
9. Early September 1938: five SNS surrounds a 40-member Arab gang assembled in the village of Beit Lidd, in the centre of the Plain of Esdraelon, to wreck the pipeline. Fourteen saboteurs are killed with two being captured along with documents.
10. Mid-September 1938: the SNS attack Beit Shean (or Beisan) in order to round up rebel suspects after the head of the Ein Harod settlement is killed by a mine.
11. 23 September 1938: the village of Danna is surrounded by the SNS on intelligence that Arab rebels infiltrating from Syria are assembling there. Twelve members of the Arab gang are killed including their leader.
12. 2 October 1938: a large Arab gang enters the ancient Jewish quarter of Tiberias and murder 19 Jews, the majority being sleeping children. Wingate, with two SNS, ambushes the gang on its exit from Tiberias killing at least 40.
13. 3 October 1938: in conjunction with the RAF, the SNS catch the remainder of the Arab gang between Dabburiya and Mt. Tabor; 14 rebels are killed.

between Dabburiya and Mount Tabor and, in a combined attack with the RAF, killed another 14. General Sir Edmund Ironside was touring Palestine and rushed to Tiberias upon hearing of the attack. There, he observed the aftermath of Wingate's ambush and expressed his approval. Ironside had now become another of Wingate's military patrons, refuting the popular image of Wingate as a 'maverick', at odds with all the Army's hierarchy.

Despite winning a DSO and having earned favourable comments from his superiors, Wingate's tenure in Palestine was waning. By October, Wingate was showing signs of mental and physical exhaustion, especially after the Tiberias attack. He made an abrupt decision to leave Palestine and to return to Britain on leave, ostensibly for personal reasons. One speculative explanation for his hasty departure from his post with the SNS was that Dr Chaim Weitzmann, one of the leading Zionists, had cabled him to return to London since political events were unfolding in Chamberlain's government after the Munich Crisis that were to undermine the cause for a Jewish homeland.

HOUR OF DESTINY

Upon his arrival in London at the end of October 1938, Wingate sought out the politically powerful to promote his belief that only through the establishment of a Jewish state in Palestine could the British government enforce permanent peace. In early November, Wingate clashed with Lord Beaverbrook, the press baron, losing his temper after only 15 minutes of discussion. Four days later, an editorial was published in Beaverbrook's *Sunday Express*, in which Wingate was indirectly chastised: 'Beware above everything

The Abyssinian guerrilla Patriot leader, Ras Garussa, who led 5,000 men against the Italians in the Jimma area of Ethiopia. (IWM, K 2966)

of catchpenny agitation stating the Jewish case in violent and offensive terms by men who really give no allegiance to Zionism and the Zionist cause but who merely embrace it for the sake of its advantage to themselves'.

Remaining undeterred in his cause, Wingate met Winston Churchill at his birthday party in London on 30 November 1938. Prior to the meeting, Wingate's memorandum on SNS theory and practice, had been forwarded to the future prime minister by Capt. Basil Liddell-Hart, the military correspondent for *The Times*. At Churchill's party, Wingate did not hesitate to discuss the political landscape in Palestine, to champion the effectiveness of the SNS and to air his strong pro-Zionist views. His meeting with both Churchill and Liddell-Hart, among others, created a firestorm: his superiors in Palestine regarded Wingate's political behaviour as improper conduct for a serving British officer.

Early in December 1938, Wingate received orders to report to GHQ in Jerusalem. He was removed from his command of the SNS, which passed to Lt. Bredin. With the Munich Crisis over, the garrison in Palestine was strengthened to 18 British infantry battalions, which produced a gradual end to the Arab Revolt. In an effort to prevent a recurrence of the Arab Rebellion, British commanders were now using Jewish troops in British uniforms on offensive raids in Palestine, and Wingate's SNS ambushes were less necessary. By January 1939, the Ein Harod SNS camp was closed and the main body, almost entirely British in composition, moved to the north where it still engaged a few Arab saboteurs. Wingate was relegated to staff duties.

Wingate's annual Confidential Report for 1938 was written by his immediate superior, Wing Commander Alan Ritchie, head of Military Intelligence in Palestine, and by Gen. Haining. The report praised Wingate's imagination and energy, but both officers criticized Wingate's attachment to the Zionist cause, and concluded that his political stance had undermined his judgement and effectiveness as an officer. Wingate took offense and wanted to exercise the right of any officer to appeal to the King over an adverse personal report. Thus, Wingate's 'lobbying', on behalf of Weitzmann in London, temporally coincided with a fall from favour.

On 26 May Wingate and his wife left Palestine. Soon thereafter, he penned his memorandum, *Palestine in Imperial Strategy*. While making port in Gibraltar, he presented this work to Ironside, then the Governor and Commander-in Chief, Gibraltar but soon to become CIGS. To demonstrate his support for the former SNS leader, Ironside wrote about Wingate on 22 August to General Henry Pownall, Director of Military Operations: 'I believe that he got a bad mark for being too Jewish. He is a most remarkable soldier and leader of men. He infused glory into his Jewish squads. If we get into war we shall want all we can find.'

On 3 September 1939, when Britain declared war on Nazi Germany, Ironside was made Chief of the Imperial General Staff, while Wingate's old sponsor, Wavell, became Commander-in-Chief, Middle East. It should be noted that on 3 November Ironside wrote a memorandum to the Secretary of State for War, Leslie Hore-Belisha: 'I consider that the appeal [by Wingate to the King] should not be allowed. I feel that there is nothing in the report [of Ritchie and Haining] which prevents Captain Wingate being employed for the good of the Army. I think that he can rest assured that his merit is thoroughly known.'

As 1939 drew to a close, Wingate decided not to pursue the appeal of his Confidential Report. The case was closed and Wingate remained in England as Adjutant, 56th Light Anti-Aircraft Brigade RA, although in early June 1940, Ironside, now Commander-in-Chief, Home Forces did interview Wingate to consider developing small guerrilla forces composed of mobile columns with Bren gun carriers and commanded by young officers should the Home Isles be invaded. In fact, Wingate raised a unit of 150 men within 24 hours from his anti-aircraft brigade; however, logistical and political hurdles prevented its ultimate formation.

In July 1940, during a meeting of the Middle East Committee of the Cabinet, Leo Amery, Secretary of State for India and Burma, suggested to Gen. Haining, now Vice-CIGS, that Wingate should lead insurgent forces in Ethiopia as part of Wavell's planned operations against Italian East Africa. Mussolini's Italy had declared war on Great Britain on 10 June. Amery was Wingate's highest-placed and one of his most enthusiastic supporters until after the first Chindit operation, when Churchill assumed this status. Amery realized that Wingate was 'not altogether easy to fit into any ordinary disciplined organization, but very much the man for a small show of his own'. In August 1940, Amery went even further and proposed that Wingate should lead 'whatever Jewish force is raised in Palestine', but when this notion was rejected, largely to placate the Palestinian Arabs, the Ethiopian enterprise was raised again. Despite his earlier differences with Wingate, Haining offered the former SNS leader to Wavell as 'suitable for leading irregulars or rebels in Abyssinia'. Wavell had apparently already cabled London to request Wingate 'to fan into flame the embers of revolt that had smouldered in parts of the Abyssinian highlands ever since the Italian occupation'.

In the distance, smoke is rising from Fort Gallabat during combat between the Italians and General Platt's forces on the Sudan-Ethiopian border, 22 November 1940. (IWM, E 1227)

To Ethiopia at Wavell's request

On 18 September 1940 Wingate was ordered to Africa, reporting to Cairo on 17 October to a department at GHQ called G (R), which was assembled to foment rebellion in Ethiopia. Wingate was forbidden to visit Palestine since his well-known views about leading a Jewish Army were not deemed helpful. Wavell, who valued Wingate's irregular warfare methods,

sent him to Khartoum to develop a force of Ethiopian rebels and Sudanese regular troops to administer 'shock therapy' to defeat the Italians in Ethiopia's Gojjam Province. Wingate arrived in Khartoum in early November as a major and GSO2 on the *kaid's* staff. His official role was delineated in a letter from Major-General William Platt, GOC Sudan (and known as *kaid*, or 'leader of the army') to Emperor Haile Selassie on 10 November. However, Wavell had been carrying out clandestine operations for over a year before Wingate's arrival.

In August 1939, Wavell sent for Lieutenant-Colonel Daniel Sandford, who had been living in England on half-pay. Sandford had worked in Ethiopia for many years and was a friend of Haile Selassie, who had lost his throne in 1936 after the Abyssinian War and was in exile in England. Sandford was promoted to colonel upon arriving in Cairo the following month and was put in charge of the Ethiopian section of the intelligence department at GHQ Middle East. He was tasked with planning an insurrection in Italian-occupied Ethiopia should hostilities develop with that Axis partner. Wavell ordered the Sudan Defence Force (SDF) to assist Sandford and soon after Italy's declaration of war, Platt sanctioned the formation of a military mission to Ethiopia, consisting of frontier supply depots and mobile radio units. Sandford, an artilleryman, based the name of his mission on that of a percussion/graze fuse, Fuse 101, which was

1. Early July 1940: Italian troops from Gondar attack British forces on the Anglo-Sudan border and occupy Kassala and Gallabat in eastern Sudan.
2. 3 August 1940: Italian troops invade British Somaliland from eastern Ethiopia, compelling the British to evacuate from Berbera to Aden across the Gulf of Aden on 19 August.
3. 12 August 1940: Sandford leads Ethiopian rebels (Mission 101) in the Gojjam Province to prevent Italian troops deploying against Platt in northern Ethiopia and Eritrea.
4. October–November 1940: ad hoc British troops (Gazelle Force) under Col. Messervy harass Italian troops along the west-to-east line of Kassala–Asmara.
5. November 1940: Maj. Orde Wingate, a GSO2 on Platt's staff, sent to Khartoum to foment rebellion in the Gojjam and seize control of the roads from Addis Ababa to Eritrea and south-west to the Kenya border. He then forms Gideon Force composed of 2,000 Sudanese and Ethiopian soldiers led by 70 British officers and NCOs.
6. 16 January 1941: elements of the 1st SA Division attack Mega inside Ethiopia then Moyale on the Kenyan frontier, the latter is abandoned by the Italians.
7. 20 January 1941: Selassie crosses the frontier and plants his flag on Ethiopian soil. Gideon Force moves into the Gojjam.
8. 6 February 1941: Wingate establishes the Emperor's HQ at Belaiya south-west of Lake Tana and then advances into the Gojjam to cut the Addis Ababa–Debra Markos road. Major Anthony Simonds moves north-east of the Gojjam towards Bahr Dar Giorgis in Beghemder Province.
9. February 1941: Cunningham's troops attack Italian Somaliland from Kenya on 6 February.
10. 1 March 1941: Cunningham starts an 850-mile advance to Harar and Dire Dawa in eastern Ethiopia to cut Italian communications

between Addis Ababa and Djibouti.
11. 6 March 1941: Italians retreating from Burye on the way towards Debra Markos, attack Wingate's 2nd Ethiopian Bn. and inflict severe casualties.
12. 16 March 1941: British troops amphibiously assault Berbera from Aden. Jijiga captured by Cunningham's forces on 17 March and his 1st SA Brigade from Mogadishu link up with the Aden force on 20 March. This combined force advances westwards towards Dire Dawa.
13. 26 March 1941: Cunningham captures Harar and three days later Dire Dawa with elements of the 1st SA Division and the 11th and 12th African Divisions.
14. Early April 1941: Gideon Force clears the whole of Gojjam between the Blue Nile and Lake Tana, opening the route for Selassie to return to the Gojjam's capital, Debra Markos.
15. 3 April 1941: Italians desert Debra Markos after a brief battle. Emperor Selassie returned to Debra Markos on 6 April. At the same time, the Duke of Aosta evacuates Addis Ababa and heads north towards the mountains of Amba Alagi.
16. 6 April 1941: Addis Ababa liberated by Cunningham after a South African Air Force bombardment the previous day. 1st SA Brigade sets out from Addis Ababa to open the main route to Asmara.
17. 5 May 1941: Selassie re-enters his capital in a captured Italian car with Wingate leading the parade on a white horse. With Selassie installed in Addis Ababa, Gideon Force joins Mission 101 in harassing the withdrawing Italian troops.
18. 23 May 1941: Italians under Col. Maraventano surrenderes a 12,000-man force to Wingate near Agibar. Platt and Cunningham's forces converge on Amba Alagi compelling the Duke of Aosta to surrender. Pockets of Italian resistance keep Cunningham's two African divisions occupied until the last Italians surrender on 27 November 1941.

Wingate's area of operations in Ethiopia during the East African campaign

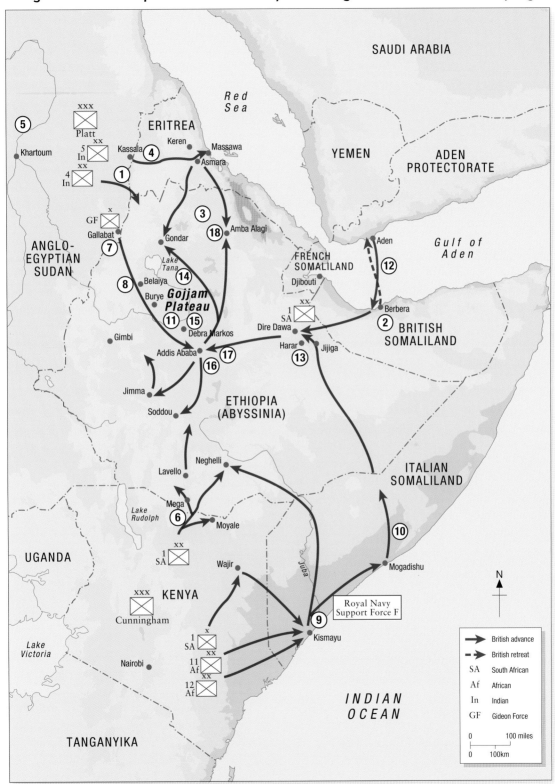

SAUDI ARABIA

Red Sea

ERITREA

YEMEN

ADEN PROTECTORATE

Khartoum

Kassala
Keren
Massawa
Asmara

Gulf of Aden

Aden

ANGLO-EGYPTIAN SUDAN

Gallabat

Gondar
Amba Alagi

FRENCH SOMALILAND

Djibouti

Lake Tana
Belaiya
Burye
Gojjam Plateau

Berbera

BRITISH SOMALILAND

Gimbi
Debra Markos
Dire Dawa
Harar
Jijiga

Addis Ababa

Jimma

Soddou

ETHIOPIA (ABYSSINIA)

ITALIAN SOMALILAND

Neghelli
Lavello

Mega
Moyale

Lake Rudolph

Mogadishu

UGANDA

Wajir

Juba

KENYA

Cunningham

Lake Victoria

Nairobi

Kismayu

Royal Navy Support Force F

N

INDIAN OCEAN

TANGANYIKA

→	British advance
⇢	British retreat
SA	South African
Af	African
In	Indian
GF	Gideon Force

0   100 miles
0   100km

Platt
5 In
4 In
GF
1 SA
1 SA
1 SA
11 Af
12 Af

Indian troops, under General Platt, advancing through an Eritrean village in early 1941. (IWM, E 2182)

British soldiers at a meal in Eritrea in March 1941. Notice the sun helmets worn by several of the troops. This headgear was to become Wingate's trademark. (IWM, E 2172)

widely used by the Royal Artillery. It was Sandford's intent that Mission 101 would 'ignite the Ethiopian revolt'. Throughout the spring of 1940, a frontier battalion was formed from cadres of the SDF and placed under the command of Lieutenant-Colonel Hugh Boustead. On 21 June, Platt issued a directive to Sandford ordering 'the entry into Abyssinia of British Mission No. 101 under Colonel Sandford who will coordinate the actions of the Abyssinians under my general direction'.

Haile Selassie landed in Khartoum on 12 August 1940, almost three months before Wingate's arrival. It was initially Sandford who insisted that Selassie must eventually return to Ethiopia to lead the revolt and reclaim his throne. Within days, Sandford led Mission 101 from the Sudan border into Ethiopia's Gojjam Province, which was the most accessible area where effective resistance had been operating against the Italians. When Wingate arrived in Khartoum on 6 November, he was to be a staff liaison officer between Mission 101, GHQ Middle East, Platt and the Emperor. However, 'Wingate lost no time in turning his staff appointment into a command'. Also, upon learning of his assignment to Khartoum, Wingate asked his former comrade from GHQ Jerusalem in 1937, Maj. Anthony Simonds, who was now at GHQ Cairo in the G(R) department, to be his second-in-command. Wingate and Selassie made an immediate strong impression on one another, with the Englishman acquiring a new cause to champion. On 20 November Wingate flew into the Gojjam to meet Sandford for the first time. Wingate reported that Mission 101 was a suitable reconnaissance force but had limited military capabilities. However, in fairness to Sandford's Mission 101, the Patriot activity that it had encouraged would eventually enable Wingate, with his combined guerrilla and regular forces, to re-enter Ethiopia with Selassie in January 1941 almost free from Italian interference. Wingate's creative energy (along with Sandford's earlier vision) enabled the development of a new British-led military unit that would fit the needs of both the local strategic mission and his patron, in this case Wavell. Both Sandford and Wingate regarded Selassie's return as a

catalyst for a national insurrection against the Italians, especially since the Gojjam Patriots had been fighting the Italian occupiers since 1937. With sufficient arms and encouragement, and with Selassie as the standard bearer, both believed that the rebels as a solitary force would be sufficient to defeat the Italians.

With garrisons situated in Ethiopia, the Italian army and local levies under the Duke of Aosta threatened the British colony of Kenya to the south, where Lieutenant-General Alan Cunningham's Southern Force was positioned,

Troops of the West African Frontier Force removing Italian monumental stones after routing the enemy in Italian Somaliland in early 1941. (IWM, E 2003)

as well as Uganda to the south-west. The duke's troops in Italian Somaliland could also advance along the Kenyan coast on the Indian Ocean. Italian-controlled Eritrea, on Ethiopia's northern border, with its Red Sea port of Massawa, was a potential staging area for attacks against both Sudan and Egypt. In aggregate, the duke had about 330,000 troops in Italian East Africa when hostilities commenced.

As early as 2 December 1940, Wavell had consulted with Cunningham and Platt to discuss his offensive strategy against the Italians. His operational plan for the Middle East had been formulated as early as July 1939, when he became C-in-C, Middle East. Wavell listed the clearing of Italian troops from the Red Sea as his second priority, only after the defence of the Suez Canal and Egypt. To achieve the objective, Wavell would have to attack in Ethiopia's central zone, the Gojjam, as well as to the north in Eritrea. After war broke out, Platt was to enter Eritrea from Kassala and oversee Wingate's force to penetrate the Gojjam from Sudan. Sandford left for the region north of the Gojjam in command of Mission 101. To further support Wingate and the Patriot rebellion, Cunningham would attack Italian Somaliland from Kenya and then pivot northward. Wavell's aim was for Cunningham to converge on Addis Ababa from the south, while Wingate advanced south-eastwards across the Gojjam to attack the Ethiopian capital.

In early January 1941, Wingate crossed the Sudan–Ethiopia border. He named his unit 'Gideon Force', after the biblical warrior Gideon, in Judges 7:7, who chose 300 men that surrounded and defeated a numerically superior Midianite army. Gideon Force was comprised of the Frontier Battalion of the SDF (under Boustead) and the 2nd Ethiopian Battalion (formerly regular soldiers of Selassie), which had previously assembled at Roseires in the Sudan. Thus, Wingate's command, which totalled about 2,000 Sudanese and Abyssinian regulars, 1,000 Abyssinian guerrillas, and an assortment of British officers and NCOs, ultimately defeated the 36,000 Italians in the Gojjam, who possessed armoured cars, field guns, bombers and fighter-planes. Wingate injected his creative leadership onto this irregular force and when his own deceptive propaganda caused the Italian troops to overestimate the size of Gideon Force, they withdrew towards the Gojjam's capital, Debra Markos. On 6 February Wingate

Men of the King's African Rifles (KAR) stacking weapons from surrendering Italians. (IWM, E 6064)

established the emperor's HQ at Belaiya, south-west of Lake Tana and then advanced further into the Gojjam to cut the Addis Ababa–Debra Markos road. The arrival at Belaiya finally gave the Emperor Haile Selassie a base in his own country from which to issue proclamations.

Sandford, meanwhile, was unaware that a change in command was afoot. He expected to continue at the head of Mission 101, with Wingate serving under him. However, on 8 February orders from Khartoum stated that Wingate was to be commander of British and Ethiopian troops in Gojjam, while Sandford was to become the military adviser to the Emperor. The new command structure produced tension in the British camp, with Wingate being promoted to lieutenant-colonel and Sandford becoming a brigadier. Essentially, orders for military operations were sent to Wingate for implementation with Gideon Force, while Sandford received copies. Sandford would then consult with Selassie to coordinate the plans and have them forwarded to the Patriot chiefs in the emperor's name. Wingate would often complain about Sandford's interference in his dispatches.

In a further development, Simonds, along with Wilfred Thesiger (of the SDF), was to move north-east of the Gojjam towards Bahr Dar Giorgis in Beghemder Province east of Lake Tana, while Wingate took over Mission 101. Though under Wingate's orders, Simond's Beghemder Force acted almost independently, with its chief goal being to prevent the Italians from reorganizing north of Gojjam and launching a flank attack on Gideon Force. Wingate's deployment of Simonds with Beghemder Force was a forerunner to his later long-range penetrations in Burma, but here in Ethiopia it would ultimately cut off the escape route of roughly 10,000 Italian troops in Dessie as the campaign wore on.

By February 1941 Cunningham commanded 77,000 troops in Kenya, which included 1st South African (SA) and the 11th and 12th African divisions. Wavell hastened Cunningham's anticipated spring southern offensive. On 6 February Cunningham's troops attacked Italian Somaliland from Kenya and on 10 February he deployed four brigade groups against the Italians on the river Juba. The British took the port of Kismayu at the mouth of the Juba without opposition on 14 February. On 25 February these forces captured Mogadishu with the assistance of the Royal Navy. On 1 March the Italians began evacuating Italian Somaliland and Cunningham started an 850-mile advance to Harar and Dire Dawa in eastern Ethiopia to cut Italian communications between Addis Ababa and Djibouti in Vichy French Somaliland. Cunningham captured Harar on 26 March, and three days later Dire Dawa, with elements of the 1st SA Division and the 11th and 12th African Divisions. On 6 April, Cunningham liberated Addis Ababa after a South African Air Force bombardment the previous day. 1st South African Brigade then set out from Addis Ababa to open the main route to Asmara, the capital of Eritrea. Much to the displeasure of both Selassie and Wingate, Cunningham was strongly opposed to the emperor entering the capital too soon.

As to Platt, his 4th Indian Division reoccupied Kassala after the Italians precipitously evacuated it on 18 January 1941. At Wavell's urging, Platt pushed up the start of his assault against Italian fortresses guarding Keren and the route to Asmara and Massawa, the port on the Red Sea. The attack stalled after six days, however, and troops of the 5th Indian Division were transported forward to resume the offensive. Eventually, Keren was assaulted on 15 March and only fell after ferocious fighting on 27 March. Asmara fell to Platt on 1 April after the Italians abandoned it. A combined British infantry and tank attack took Massawa on 8 April, opening the Red Sea. It had always been Wavell's ultimate goal to transfer some of Cunningham's South African troops to the Western Desert via Massawa or overland through the Sudan.

On 27/28 February, Wingate's 1,500 troops were poised to advance against two colonial brigades, while Beghemder Force pursued a third brigade northwards. It would seem that in the overall scheme of Platt and Cunningham's pincer movement into Eritrea and Italian Somaliland, Wingate's advances would be a small component. When examined closely, however, the movement of Gideon Force did serve to rally the Ethiopian patriots against formidable odds. Wingate fought the Italians at Burye followed by a running engagement over three days at Mankusa, which forced yet another Italian withdrawal. However, on 6 March, while marching on the road to Debra Markos, the Ethiopian Battalion was overwhelmed by a much larger, retreating Italian force at Dambacha. Wingate occupied Dambacha on 8 March. The Italian commander, recognizing that he had

General Sir Alan Cunningham who led the southern pincer through Italian Somaliland and Ethiopia. After the Italian surrender, Cunningham ordered Wingate out of Ethiopia. (IWM, E 6661)

been deceived as to the strength of Wingate's detachment, stiffened his troops' resistance. On 11 March, Wingate and Gideon Force marched from Dambacha in pursuit of the Italians. With each successive move by Wingate into the Gojjam, Sandford and Emperor Selassie's column followed. Debra Markos fell on 3 April, enabling Wingate to acquire his first objective and Emperor Selassie to enter Gojjam's capital three days later. At the end of the first week of April 1941, Platt's Indian troops were in Asmara, while Cunningham's had captured Addis Ababa. Part of Gideon Force continued to pursue Colonel Maraventano, the Italian commander in the Gojjam.

The month prior to Selassie's entry into the capital was a frustrating one for Wingate. He had quarrelled with Sandford when he volunteered the use of Gideon Force in the operations now taking place to the north around Lake Tana in Gondar, but was ordered not to get involved. Wingate also annoyed Platt, the commander of the British advance in Eritrea in 1941, because the Gideon Force leader believed the British government was lukewarm about the guerrilla achievements, and wanted British regular forces to enter the capital first and so diminish the emperor's prestige. Platt also expressed general disdain for covert operations and irregular forces, and was no friend of Wingate stating, 'The curse of this war is Lawrence in the last'.

On 5 May Selassie re-entered his capital in a captured Italian car, with Wingate leading the parade on a white horse. Selassie's entry into Addis Ababa had a dual importance. First, it demonstrated to the Ethiopians from both political and symbolic standpoints, that their emperor had, indeed, been returned to his throne. Second, he needed to get to his capital to raise an army to pursue the Italians, as Wavell transferred many of Platt and Cunningham's imperial troops to North Africa to confront the eastward advance of Rommel's Afrika Korps.

With Selassie installed in Addis Ababa, Gideon Force's campaign was not yet over. Wingate was ordered to take part of Gideon Force and join Mission 101, which was harassing the withdrawing Italian troops. The Italians who had been forced out of Debra Markos were cut off from the Duke of Aosta's other troops by the capture of Addis Ababa. As they were making their way across country, Safartak Force (abbreviated to Safforce), a detachment of the Frontier Battalion, harassed them. The retreating Italians established a strong position at Addis Derra, which Safforce, reinforced by 2,000 Patriots, could not penetrate. Wingate arrived on 14 May only to be ordered by Cunningham on the following day to break up Gideon Force. Wingate was insubordinate and ignored Cunningham's instructions by turning off his radio. However, when he prepared to attack the following day, the Italians evacuated and moved to a new defensive position at Agibar, 30 miles to the north. Wingate, along with his SDF subordinate Thesiger, forced the

Italians to withdraw from their redoubt over the next three days. On 20 May Wingate sent Maraventano a letter informing him of the surrender of the Duke of Aosta at Amba Alagi the previous day and gave him 24 hours to surrender to British troops or be confronted by Patriot forces. The terms of surrender were negotiated by representatives of Wingate and Maraventano on 22 May. The following day, a column of 10,000 enemy troops surrendered to a considerably smaller force commanded by Wingate. According to Shirreff, 'The Patriots tackled the greatly superior forces of the Maraventano column with reckless courage, and without their sacrifice Wingate's bluff in bringing about the surrender of the column would not have succeeded.... While it is right to praise the Patriots, the plan and direction was Wingate's. The whole operation was a good example of the support of guerrilla forces by a regular nucleus, and bringing about the surrender of the column as Wingate's most spectacular in Ethiopia'.

Wingate confers with the Emperor Haile Selassie during the Gideon Force campaign in the Gojjam in early 1941. (IWM, E 1647)

William Allen, a captain in Wingate's Gideon Force wrote, 'Gideon Force had to trek across western Ethiopia through thick scrub and rocky, thorny wadis, climb a 3,000-foot rock wall to a plateau, and endure heat, a shortage of water, jaundice, dysentery, malaria, and parasite flea infections. Dense clouds of flies hovered overhead. Camels died at a rate of over 50 a day. Vultures so fattened themselves on the carcasses that they stumbled about, too heavy to get airborne'. Allen further noted that Wingate 'never spared

Lieutenant-General Alan Cunningham welcoming the Emperor Haile Selassie back to his capital, Addis Ababa in May 1941. Although Cunningham had entered the capital the previous month, he argued that it was unsafe for the Emperor to return then, which Wingate disputed, suspecting political motives. (IWM, E 3035)

his own body.... Some demon chased Wingate over the highlands.... His pale blue eyes, narrow-set, burned with an insatiable glare. His spare, bony, ugly figure with its crouching gait had the hang of animal run by hunting yet hungry for the next night's prey.'

Using tactics similar to those he had employed against the Arab gangs in Palestine, Wingate panicked the Italian troops by using his sentries as snipers during the darkness, and sending small groups out to launch hand-grenade attacks. As noted by Captain Allen,

> A mortar fire, maintained during the night, was directed against the fort, and by the morning the majority of the buildings within the fort area were burning. Machine-gun fire throughout the whole of the second day; while from time to time native propagandists from loudspeakers harangued the Colonial troops within. The morale of the garrison of the fort began to sag as deserters began to find their way to the Patriot bands covering the road against any breakout to the west.

Wingate also excelled in the art of military deception, repeatedly deceiving his opposing commanders as to his strength, compelling the enemy to make hasty, incorrect decisions.

On 1 June Wingate reported to Lieutenant-General Sir Harry Wetherall, Cunningham's deputy, at Addis Ababa. Wetherall informed Wingate that Gideon Force was being disbanded and that he was to fly to Cunningham's HQ at Harar. Cunningham accepted Wingate's explanation for his disobedience at Addis Derra, but ordered him to leave Ethiopia immediately. It should be emphasized that Wingate did not engage in politics in Ethiopia, leaving those matters to Sandford.

Wingate flew to Khartoum and then on to Cairo with his old rank of major. Very bitter about the lack of recognition for his accomplishments with Gideon Force, Wingate took out his frustrations in a memorandum that was highly critical of his superiors. After Wavell read the report, he concluded that it would have justified Wingate's arrest for insubordination, but he took the trouble to meet him to address the issues. Wavell was critical of Wingate's indiscreet language, but promised to investigate the grievances listed, chief among them decorations requested but not awarded. However, Wavell was soon to be sacked as C-in-C Middle East and was to leave for India on 7 July to take up the same post on the subcontinent.

On 4 July Wingate attempted to commit suicide in his hotel room by cutting his throat. He was found by an officer in the next room, who took him to the hospital before he bled to death. In fact, Wingate was delirious from the effects both of cerebral malaria and of an overdose of the drug he was taking to combat it (atabrine, which can cause depression as a side effect). He had just finished a

Brigadier Daniel Sandford (left) and Colonel Wingate (right) flank Emperor Haile Selassie in Dambacha Fort in the Gojjam Province after it had been captured by Gideon Force. (IWM, E 2462)

formidable campaign under very harsh conditions in Ethiopia and had not received the praise he had expected from his superiors. In Cairo, the ambivalence towards him at GHQ persisted, thus his anger and frustration during an attack of cerebral malaria swayed his volatile mental status toward the path of suicide. On 22 July a psychiatric assessment deemed that the suicide attempt was the consequence of 'a depressed state to which he was prone, aggravated by malarial fever'. The medical report concluded that he was no longer suicidal and had fully recovered his mental faculties.

Ethiopian camel troops moving supplies through dense terrain in January 1941. (IWM, E 1715)

Wingate was evacuated to England in mid-November. Back home, he met up again with Amery, under whose guidance Wingate modified his report to remove all the offensive passages. Amery passed the amended memorandum to the new CIGS, General Sir Alan Brooke, among others. There were no repercussions from Wingate's report and he was passed fit for active service by a medical board on 30 December 1941. On 7 February 1942, he received orders to proceed to Wimborne to take command of a battery in 114th Regiment, RA.

Two officers demonstrated the contrasting views of Wingate's performance in Ethiopia. The first was Wetherall, Cunningham's deputy, who wrote about Wingate's operations in western Ethiopia in 1941: 'This brilliant action... as a feat of arms carried out by a minute regular force supporting irregulars in very difficult country against an enemy greatly superior in numbers and armament can have few parallels'. The other officer, Wilfred Thesiger, Wingate's subordinate from the SDF, who appreciated but disliked the Gideon Force commander, commented: 'Wingate took me round various offices at Headquarters. As he shambled from one to another, in his creased, ill-fitting uniform and out-of-date Wolseley helmet, carrying an alarm clock instead of wearing a watch, and a fly-whisk instead of a cane, I could sense the irritation and resentment he left in his wake. His behaviour certainly exasperated [General Sir William]

Upon Emperor Selassie's return to Addis Ababa in May 1941, Ethiopian warriors gather with captured Italian arms. (IWM K 325)

Platt'. It would continue to be a pattern that critics of Wingate would most often single out his demeanour and personality, rather than the military concepts or outcomes he achieved.

In sum, Gideon Force, the *corps d'élite*, was, indeed, the creation of Wingate. He laid down a conceptual framework in the Gojjam Highlands that he expanded during Burmese LRP operations, by which an independent self-contained force could interfere with enemy communications, and by use of guerrilla tactics, could ultimately force a numerically superior

enemy to withdraw, as was achieved at Burye. Wingate's expedition into the Gojjam with Gideon Force was, thus, the precursor to his first Chindit mission, Operation *Longcloth*, in Burma in 1943.

Disaster in Burma, 1942

When Wavell became C-in-C, India, he was disturbed by the lack of morale among his forces in the Far East. The Japanese advance in south-east Burma had been swift and it appeared that the British–Indian defence along the Sittang River was collapsing. Rangoon was in jeopardy and its evacuation imminent. It was Amery, again, who had informed Wavell that Wingate was fit and available for active service. Wavell, who always favoured unorthodoxy and had been impressed by Gideon Force's performance in Ethiopia, summoned Wingate to Burma to join his staff. Wavell believed that Wingate's methods might help stem the unstoppable Japanese advance in Burma. Wingate flew to Delhi arriving on 19 March 1942.

Wavell wanted Wingate to organize operations against Japanese lines of communication. Rangoon had fallen and Wingate, with his rank of colonel restored, was sent to Maymyo, in Burma, to take command of guerrilla operations. On arrival Gen. Hutton told him that there was little chance to expand guerrilla activities because of a shortage of personnel and *matériel*, as well as the impressive speed of the Imperial Japanese Army (IJA) advance. Instead, Wingate was told to meet Major Michael Calvert at his Bush Warfare School. Calvert was a sapper who had fought the Germans in Norway, helped run the Commando training centre at Lochailort and was instructing British officers to lead Chinese guerrillas against the Japanese in China. Wingate also met with Burcorps' commander, Gen. Slim, at Prome and flew to Chungking to consult the British Military Mission. In his aircraft was Generalissimo Chiang Kai-Shek and the two discussed guerrilla-style tactics with Chinese troops during the air journey. However, the deteriorating situation impeded Wingate's ability to direct the guerrilla units that were formed in Burma, since the Japanese had advanced to the Chindwin River on India's frontier.

General Sir Claude Auchinleck (left) and Field Marshal Sir Archibald Wavell (right) conferring over a map. Wavell was C-in-C India, with Auchinleck as his deputy when Wingate was implementing Operation *Longcloth* in 1943. By the time of Operation *Thursday*, a year later, Wavell had become Viceroy of India, with Auchinleck becoming C-in-C India. Auchinleck clashed with Wingate about the personnel requirements for 3rd Indian Division or Special Force. (IWM, E 5450)

Wingate returned to Delhi at the end of April 1942 and wrote a memorandum to Wavell on 'Long Range Penetration' (LRP). He stated that radio communications and air-supply would allow him to penetrate into the enemy's interior. Burma's jungle canopy and mountains would obscure his force's movements and would, thus, be a perfect theatre to test LRP methods to disrupt Japanese communications. GHQ in Delhi had begun to pare down Wingate's proposed mission even before Wavell had given his final approval. Chief among the adversaries to Wingate's operations was Major-General S. Woodburn Kirby, the Director of Staff Duties, who was responsible for allocating troops. Nonetheless, Wavell approved Wingate's proposal because he trusted his unorthodox methods.

In July 1942 77th Indian Brigade was formed with troops from the 13th King's Liverpool Regiment as a nucleus. It was an odd choice, since this regiment had been on coastal defence duties in England prior to transfer to India to serve primarily as garrison troops. Ironically, most had lived in large urban centres such as Liverpool and Manchester and the average age was over 30. Many were married, while others were physically unsuitable for the rigorous training regimen Wingate had planned. After some serious culling of the ranks, 77th Indian Brigade was to be made up of eight columns, originally of 400 men each, which was based on an infantry company's size. However, Column 6 had to be broken up to replace casualties incurred in training among the other seven columns. Half of the columns were Gurkhas, the others British. The 3rd/2nd Gurkha Rifles were formed largely of under-age recruits with inexperienced officers and NCOs. The understrength 2nd Burma Rifles were seasoned troops, and also supplied reconnaissance platoons for the other columns. The Sabotage Group, 142 Commando Company, well-trained demolition experts and survivors of Calvert's Bush Warfare School, were distributed among the columns. A major commanded each column. The SMLE rifle, Bren gun, Boys anti-tank rifle, Vickers medium machine gun and Thompson sub-machine gun were among the usual infantry weapons utilized by Wingate's force. There was no heavy transport, and mules carried the heavier equipment. Since air-supply was of paramount importance, an RAF signal section was attached to each column to direct British aircraft to suitable parachute dropping zones. The term, 'Chindit', now entrenched in military lore, was derived from Wingate's misunderstanding of the pronunciation of the Burmese word for lion, 'Chinthe', the supreme animal of the Burma jungle.

After months of training for the first Chindit mission, Operation *Longcloth*, a strategic hurdle appeared in early February 1943 that almost cancelled it. Wavell had intended to send 77th Indian Brigade into Burma by foot in advance of an assault by IV Corps from Assam across the Chindwin River. These British operations were to temporally coincide with two Chinese offensives, one mounted from China's Yunnan province and the other a Sino-American effort, under General Stilwell, entering Burma south from Ledo in north-east Assam. Wingate's mission was to support these operations by disrupting Japanese communications, principally by destroying large portions of the railway to the west of the Irrawaddy River. After that, Wingate intended 77th Indian Brigade to cross the Irrawaddy to

The monocled Maj. Bernard Fergusson after leading Column 5 during Operation *Longcloth*. He was promoted to brigadier and led 16th Brigade on its overland march from Ledo to Indaw during Operation *Thursday*. (IWM, KY 471212A)

further disrupt Japanese communications on the Salween River front, where the Chinese forces in Yunnan were to advance. The Chinese invasions of Burma, which were out of Wavell's control, as well as IV Corps' offensive, were all cancelled in early 1943, which would logically stall Operation *Longcloth* on 3 February. Only the Arakan offensive of 1943 was to go ahead as planned. GHQ in Delhi believed that a Chindit invasion of central Burma alone would fail and would also alert the Japanese to Stilwell's ultimate intentions in northern Burma. Wavell, always Wingate's dutiful patron, went to Imphal to discuss the situation with him on 7 February.

Wavell approved the departure of Operation *Longcloth* from Imphal on 8 February after a spirited debate in which Wingate offered six major points to support his contention as to how his LRP force alone could provide a meaningful strategic endpoint.

1) It would be a vital chance to mission- and field-test his ideas.
2) Cancellation would shatter the élan that had developed in 77th Indian Brigade.
3) Operation *Longcloth* would test whether the Burmese would assist the British to evict the Japanese from their country.
4) The Chindit LRP would reduce the pressure of a Japanese offensive on Fort Hertz, the last British bastion in Burma.
5) The Chindit operation could disrupt Japanese infiltration across the Chindwin River into India.
6) Operation *Longcloth* might pre-empt any Japanese offensive against Assam in 1943.

According to Wavell,

> I had to balance the inevitable losses – the larger since there would be no other operations to divide the enemy's forces – to be sustained without strategical profit, against the experience to be gained of Wingate's new method and organization. I had little doubt in my own mind of the proper course, but I had to satisfy myself also that Wingate had no doubts and that the enterprise had a good chance of success and would not be a senseless sacrifice… and I went into Wingate's proposals in some detail before giving the sanction to proceed for which he and his brigade were so anxious.

Wingate needed Operation *Longcloth* to validate his military theories, which were on a much larger scale than those in the Sudan, Palestine, or Ethiopia. As an aside, in Burma there would be no political cause for Wingate to champion as he had earlier in the Middle East.

Operation *Longcloth*

Wingate's 77th Indian Brigade was divided into two groups: the Northern Group consisted of the Brigade HQ, the Burma Rifles HQ, HQ 2 Group and Columns 3, 4, 5, 7 and 8. The Southern Group was composed of HQ 1 Group along with Columns 1 and 2. The total strength of the Northern Group was 2,200 men, while the Southern Group had 1,000 men. 77th Indian Brigade

Chindits crossing a river in Burma during Operation *Longcloth* in 1943. (IWM, IND 2290)

was to advance between the 18th and 33rd Japanese divisions. The Southern Group, typical for Wingate, was to deceive the Japanese about 77th Indian Brigade's real intentions. While Wingate was with the Northern Group, it was rumoured that an officer disguised as Wingate himself crossed the Chindwin with the Southern Group. For Wingate's 3,000-man incursion into Burma, the strategic aim was to disrupt the lines of communication of these two Japanese divisions, specifically by demolishing the Burmese railway, which supplied them. In addition it was a critical test of his LRP philosophy and tactics.

It was Wingate's tactical construct that each of his columns should march independently, with the ability to sustain their trek for one week before radioing the RAF for air resupply. Furthermore, Wingate believed that a column's security was in its mobility and ability to disperse and regroup if confronted by larger enemy forces. However, once the fog of war descended during combat, dispersal frequently resulted in chaos when it proved impossible to brief everyone on the rendezvous to which every man should head. In principle, the absence of wheeled transport and lines of communication were positive features; however, it made supply by parachute drop an imperative for Operation *Longcloth*. Wingate also suggested that during at least the initial portion of his mission, before reaching the Irrawaddy, the camouflage offered by the jungles and teak forests of northern Burma would be a strong asset. Another tactical thread to all of Wingate's plans was the manoeuvre of 'feint and thrust'. To exemplify this, when the Southern Group feigned the main crossing of the Chindwin, the Japanese countered with a move west to Homalin, which thereby enabled Wingate's Northern group to thrust eastward into the Mu River valley towards Pinbon and Pinlebu to get behind the enemy and avoid a pitched battle.

On 13–14 February, Wingate started to cross the Chindwin River. Wingate's main body (Northern Group) crossed the Chindwin River at Tonhe, where the river was only 366m (400 yards) wide. The entire Northern Group had crossed the Chindwin by 18 February. The diversionary force (Southern Group) did so 50 miles to the south near Auktaung. The Southern Group's crossing continued until the early morning of 16 February. Its intent was to draw attention away from the main effort in the north. The Japanese never discovered 77th Indian Brigade while they were crossing the Chindwin. The Southern Group (Columns 1 and 2), commanded by Lt. Col. Alexander, made the first encounter with a small Japanese force at Maingnyaung on 18 February. After losing many pack animals, which produced a delay of three days, this group moved eastwards again.

Despite Wingate's secrecy, the Japanese had uncovered the Chindits' order of battle following an inadvertent air drop and drew in their patrols eastward and evacuated all outposts to concentrate more centrally. Wingate had decided to shift his attack on the railway from Indaw to the Wuntho area, 35 miles to the south. The Northern Group (Columns 3, 4, 5, 7, and 8), under both Wingate and Lt. Col. Cooke, moved over rough terrain for two weeks undetected by the Japanese until they concentrated near Pinbon and north of Pinlebu. Columns 3 and 5 of the Northern Group led by Maj. Calvert and Maj. Fergusson, respectively, were to head for the Wuntho–Indaw section of the Burmese railway, which ran north–south from Myitkyina to Mandalay,

1. 8 February 1943: 77th Brigade leaves Imphal to launch Operation *Longcloth*.
2. 13–14 February 1943: Wingate's main body (Northern Group) crosses the Chindwin River at Tonhe. The diversionary force (Southern Group) crosses 50 miles to the south near Auktaung.
3. 18 February 1943: Elements of the Southern Group attempt an ambush of a Japanese garrison at Maingnyaung.
4. 24/25 February 1943: Columns 3, 7 and 8 raid the deserted Japanese camp at Sinlamaung.
5. 1 March 1943: The Northern Group enter into the Chaunggyi Valley and camps near Pinbon. Here Wingate called a conference to plan the separation of Columns for individual tasks and to rendezvous beyond the Irrawaddy.
6. 2 March 1943: Southern Group's Column 2 is ambushed by a Japanese company and forced to disperse and head back to India. Column 2 ceases to exist.
7. 4 March 1943: Column 4 ambushed south-west of Pinbon and a dispersal of this Column is ordered. Unable to regroup with Wingate's Columns 7 and 8, this column withdraws to India.
8. 4–6 March 1943: Columns 7 and 8 lead a feint attack on Pinlebu further confusing the Japanese as to Wingate's intentions for the invasion.
9. 6 March 1943: Demolition of rails and railway bridges starts with Calvert's Column 3 attacking the railway line and bridges around the Nankan railway station while Fergusson's Column 5 destroys a railway bridge and blocks the railway line about 10 miles north-east at Bongyaung by dynamiting a nearby gorge.
10. 8 March 1943: Column 1 of the Southern Group crosses the Irrawaddy at Tagaung.
11. 10 March 1943: Column 5 under Fergusson reaches and crosses the Irrawaddy at Tigyaing.
12. 13 March 1943: Column 3 begins crossing the Irrawaddy 5 miles down river from Tigyaing.
13. 13 March 1943: Wingate in command of 1,200 men (Columns 7 and 8 plus two HQ groups) leaves the Bambwe Taung Hills and crosses the railway and the Meza River without meeting the enemy.
14. 17 March 1943: Wingate ordered Columns 7 and 8 along with his two HQ groups to advance to the Irrawaddy, which was crossed uneventfully on March 18th just south of Inywa.
15. 21 March 1943: After 3 days of marching 30 miles south-south-east of Inywa, Wingate's Northern Group bivouacs for two days to concentrate his straggled columns and rest his troops.
16. 24 March 1943: Calvert's Column 3 ordered to return to the Chindwin if possible via Lake Indawgyi, 60 miles north of Katha, where Wingate hoped to organize 77th Indian Brigade's rendezvous.
17. 24 March 1943: Wingate sends a cryptic Biblical message to the Southern Group (Column 1) to head for the Kachin Hills.
18. 27 March 1943: Wingate orders the remainder of the Northern Group back to India via Hinta and Inywa.
19. 29 March 1943: Wingate attempts to re-cross the Irrawaddy at Inywa with Brigade HQ and Columns 7 and 8 as well as Northern Group HQ.
20. 30 March 1943: Wingate divides his 220 men into five 'dispersal groups' and orders them back to India by any means.

Wingate's area of operations in Burma during Operation *Longcloth*, February 1943

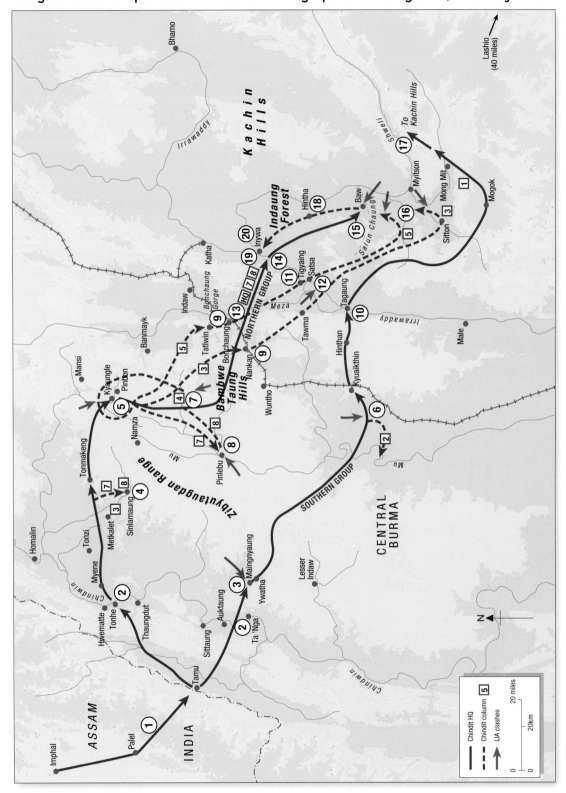

A column of weary Chindits marches through a Burmese village during Operation *Longcloth* in 1943. (IWM, SE 7911)

and cut the line in as many places as possible. The other columns were to search for and engage the Japanese concentrated near Pinbon and Pinlebu, thereby constituting 'feints' for the 'thrust' to the railway north of Wuntho by Calvert and Fergusson.

On 2 March, disaster befell Southern Group's Column 2 when a Japanese company ambushed it with accurate mortar fire and forced it to disperse. Column 2 never re-formed and, thus, ceased to exist. Column 1 reached the railway just north of Kyaikthin on 3 March and began nighttime bridge demolitions. On 4 March Column 4 was ambushed near Pinbon. Again, pack animals were stampeded and some of the younger Gurkha recruits fled the ambush site. Despite attempts at rendezvous, further Japanese attacks prevented Column 4 from rejoining the Northern Group. Without communication equipment, food, and a scant amount of ammunition their commander, Maj. Bromhead, was compelled to retreat with his column's survivors back to India. Two of Wingate's original seven columns were deleted from his order of battle. Undeterred, Column 8, under Major Scott, demonstrated against Pinlebu.

By 6 March Calvert's Column 3 had cut the railway line in 70 places, and two bridges had been destroyed, one of which had a 300ft span. Fergusson's Column 5 destroyed a railway bridge about 10 miles north-east at Bongyaung, with its 40ft centre span dropping into the river below. Fergusson also blocked the railway line by dynamiting a gorge outside Bongyaung. This section of the railway wound through the middle of northern Burma, providing the Japanese with an excellent means of communication for supply and reinforcement in an inhospitable terrain. Despite this demolition, the Japanese restored the railway line within four weeks of its destruction, using forced labour.

Chindit sappers set their demolition charges on railway tracks and the bridge supports during Operation *Longcloth* in 1943. (IWM, SE 7921)

Calvert's Column 3 did run into some Japanese resistance, but these troops were handled by his use of ambush and covering parties on the road north and south, as well as by setting booby traps. This activity enabled the demolition squads to set their charges. Two truckloads of Japanese were ambushed coming up from Wuntho, but they put up a stiff fight against Calvert's small party which was armed with a Boys anti-tank rifle, a Bren gun, and mines. Explosions were heard on the railway around 3:30pm. The Japanese were reinforced, but in the end they broke off and fled into the jungle north of Nankan. Column 3 did not lose a single Chindit during this day of fighting and railway destruction, while many Japanese were slaughtered in the open country.

Wingate's decision to cross the Irrawaddy is the most controversial of his career: it was extremely dangerous and resulted in many casualties. His main objective, the demolition of the railway had been achieved, however. According to a biographer, Christopher Sykes, 'In the incalculable way of war Wingate's decision, for all its defiance of ordinary sense, and for all the suffering it entailed, was the right one… he wanted to be the leader of such an expedition as would alter the whole tide of affairs in the most distressed and unhopeful British military theatre', which Burma had become. Unfortunately, for Wingate's legacy, certain generals at GHQ, such as Kirby, who were to write the *British Official History of the War* would blame him ceaselessly for this decision to cross the Irrawaddy because of the 'adverse topographical and climatic conditions his columns would meet to the east of it'. The specific operational dilemma for Wingate was whether crossing the Irrawaddy was more hazardous than taking his depleted columns in a reverse course through jungle country, which was now teeming with Japanese patrols. Finally, it must be stated that when Wavell re-approved Operation *Longcloth*, his orders specifically provided for 77th Indian Brigade's crossing of the Irrawaddy as long as it appeared possible, in order to evaluate and test the limits of long range penetration.

An RAF transport parachutes supplies to Chindits in the Burmese jungle well behind IJA lines. (IWM, KY471207)

On 8 March Column 1 of the Southern Group began crossing the Irrawaddy at Tagaung, which would be completed by 10 March. Wingate signalled Calvert and Fergusson from his HQ area north of Wuntho in the Bambwe Taung Hills asking them if they considered it more prudent to retire to the mountains above Wuntho to form a redoubt, or to go on eastwards across the river. Both agreed to cross the Irrawaddy without delay. On 10 March Column 5 under Fergusson reached and crossed the Irrawaddy at Tigyaing, but the Japanese had discovered their whereabouts. Calvert's Column 3 began crossing the Irrawaddy during the early morning hours of 13 March, 5 miles down river from Tigyaing, where the west shore of the Irrawaddy is divided into islands stiff with elephant grass. After a firefight with a Japanese patrol from Tawma, his crossing in commandeered Burmese boats continued until midnight. On the same day, Wingate led 1,200 men (Columns 7 and 8 plus two HQ groups) from the Bambwe Taung Hills and crossed the railway and the Meza River without meeting the enemy. On 17 March Wingate ordered Columns 7 and 8 along with his two HQ groups to advance to the Irrawaddy, which was crossed uneventfully on the following day just south of Inywa, where the formidable river is joined by its principal northern tributary, the Shweli. Wingate also issued orders on the same day for Southern Group's Column 1 to move to Mogok and then Mong

Mit. He also ordered Calvert to take Column 3 to demolish the Gokteik viaduct on the main Maymyo–Lashio road, which was not accomplished.

Once across the Irrawaddy, Wingate discovered that the country lacked cover and shade and was intensely hot with a paucity of fresh water. Knowing their whereabouts, the Japanese began to converge on the Chindit force. Fleetingly, Wingate thought of continuing his eastward movement into the Kachin Hills, which he had actively begun to reconnoitre with a platoon of the Burma Rifles, but his base in Assam had signalled that such a move would put his force outside the range of future RAF parachute drops. On 21 March, after three days of marching 30 miles south-south-east of Inywa, Wingate's Northern Group bivouacked for two days on the seasonal Salin Chang River to concentrate his straggled columns and rest his troops. Having not yet received his orders to withdraw westward to India, Calvert attacked the enemy near Sitton on 23 March, killing over 100 Japanese troops who were establishing patrol stations on the roads towards the Irrawaddy. That same day, Wingate signalled Fergusson to meet him at a supply-dropping rendezvous in the vicinity of Baw, where the 77th Indian Brigade had fought their last battle, albeit under adverse conditions. On 24 March Wingate complied with an order to recross the Irrawaddy and commence a withdrawal to the Chindwin. With the Japanese present on the west bank of the river in force and only a few boats available, this was a daunting prospect. The surviving columns were dispersed into smaller groups to achieve the crossing.

Calvert's Column 3 was ordered to return to the Chindwin if possible via Lake Indawgyi, 60 miles north of Katha, where Wingate hoped to organize 77th Indian Brigade's rendezvous. On the same day Wingate sent, not uncharacteristically, a cryptic Biblical message to his Southern Group (Column 1) to 'Remember Lot's wife. Return not whence ye came. Seek thy salvation in the mountains. Genesis XIX'. Column 1 left the area between

Railway bridge demolition by Calvert's Column 3 at Nankan, Operation *Longcloth*, 6 March 1943

Columns 3 and 5 of 77th Indian Brigade's Northern Group, led by majors Calvert and Fergusson, respectively, were to head for the Wuntho–Indaw section of the Burmese railway and cut the line in as many places as possible. Sappers of Calvert's Column 3 placed their demolition charges on the track and supports of a railway bridge spanning a mostly dry waterway near the Nankan railway station. Three other Chindits marched off to nearby ambush sites to place booby traps and confront expected IJA attacks armed with a Boys anti-tank rifle, a Thompson sub-machine gun and mines. Calvert's placement of these ambush parties astride the nearby road enabled the demolition squads to set their charges off. Two lorry-loads of Japanese were ambushed coming up from Wuntho, while other IJA troops broke off and fled into the jungle north of Nankan. Column 3 did not lose a single Chindit during this day of fighting and railway destruction. Although Calvert's men cut the railway line in over 70 places, it took only weeks for the Japanese to make the railway operational again.

Major-General Wingate looking extremely tired after his return from Burma to Assam after Operation *Longcloth*.
(IWM, JAR 2161)

Mogok and Mong Mit for the Kachin Hills. On 27 March Wingate ordered the remainder of the Northern Group back to India via Hinta and, then, Inywa. The 'Shweli loop' was a formidable trap from which to break out. On 29 March Wingate attempted to recross the Irrawaddy at Inywa with Brigade HQ and Columns 7 and 8, as well as Northern Group HQ, but after a Japanese attack from the western shore, only a portion of the force made it across the river. The next day Wingate, still south of the Shweli River on the east shore of the Irrawaddy, divided his 220 men into five 'dispersal groups' and ordered them back to India by any means.

Calvert's column returned to Assam on 15 April, with Fergusson's Column 5 on 25 April. Colonel Cooke with 16 of Northern Group's HQ had been flown back into India on 28 April after Maj. Scott coaxed the pilot to land in order to evacuate casualties. Only 34 of Wingate's 43 men made it back to Assam on 28 April after recrossing the Chindwin. Of the four dispersal groups of Brigade HQ only one, the defence platoon, reached safety. On 14 May Column 8 crossed the upper Chindwin at Tamanthi, and the HQ column of the Burma Rifles reached Fort Hertz. On the same day the remains of the Southern Group recrossed the Chindwin near Auktaung. Only 260 out of the 1,000 men in the Southern Group that left Imphal returned. Of the 3,000 men who crossed the Chindwin between 13 and 18 March, 2,182 returned to India often in small groups.

Debates continue about the merits or otherwise of Operation *Longcloth*. However, at this stage of the Allied effort to regain a successful offensive momentum against the Japanese in southern Asia, an operation of this size was remarkable by any standards. Lasting over six weeks behind IJA lines before being ordered to withdraw proved some of Wingate's theories and established training methods for subsequent missions. As historian Louis Allen stated, 'What the press and world opinion made of Wingate's initial exploits infused a new spirit into the affairs of Burma; whatever the strategic upshot, whatever Wingate's psychological faults that renewal of spirit cannot be gainsaid'. The Burma theatre needed a hero.

Operation *Thursday*

Upon Wingate's return to India, he learned that his supporter, Wavell, was to become India's viceroy, while General Sir Claude Auchinleck was to be the new Commander-in-Chief, India. To demonstrate that he still believed in LRP, Wavell ordered the conversion of the 111th Indian Brigade to LRP duties. This LRP formation was to be composed of elements of the Cameronians, the Gurkha Rifles and the King's Own Regiment, under the command of Brigadier William Lentaigne, DSO, who had earned a reputation as a courageous Gurkha commander during the Burma retreat. However, Lentaigne differed from Wingate in that he was much more orthodox, disciplined, and intelligent 'but not of outstanding imagination'.

Ever the self-promoter, Wingate had sent Amery, his political patron, his uncensored report of Operation *Longcloth*, which was written while convalescing in June 1943. This memorandum ultimately arrived on the Prime Minister's desk. The overall situation in Burma had so troubled Churchill that he had suggested

A Burmese railway bridge behind Japanese lines in central Burma explodes after Chindit sappers laid demolition charges. (IWM SE 7924)

to General Sir Hastings Ismay, 'I consider Wingate should command the army in Burma.... There is no doubt that in the welter of inefficiency and lassitude which has characterized our operations on the Indian front this man, his force and achievements, stand out, and no mere question of seniority must obstruct the advance of real personalities to their proper stations in war. He too should come home for discussion here at an early date'. However, the CIGS, General Sir Alan Brooke, convinced Churchill not to appoint Wingate to lead the new Fourteenth Army.

Reaching London on 4 August, Wingate was taken by Churchill to Quebec for the Quadrant Conference. He presented his views about an enlarged LRP expedition for Burma in 1944, as part of a multi-pronged Allied offensive in southern Asia, to the Combined Chiefs of Staff and President Roosevelt. Thanks to the interest of Roosevelt and his subordinates, the US Army was to train their own LRP force under Wingate, as well as form an Air Commando from USAAF cadres to provide the Chindits with an expanded aerial dimension to their tactical doctrine. Wingate suggested expanding the Chindits by eight brigades, with accompanying air assets. Auchinleck and his GHQ Delhi staff balked at the decision, believing that an expansion to six brigades would dismantle divisions currently training and overwhelm the available air transport available in India. Wingate, by having the support of Churchill, Roosevelt and the Chiefs of Staff, had deeply irritated Auchinleck and his GHQ. On his return to India, Wingate

Wingate (centre) with Slim (on the left) and Brig. Derek Tulloch (on the right) confer with Brig. Gen. Old (USAAF) on 5 March 1944, the starting date for Operation *Thursday*. (IWM, MH 7881)

was promoted to major-general in command of Special Force, the new title for the Chindits, with his old friend Derek Tulloch becoming his brigadier general staff. The development of Special Force proceeded slowly, but ultimately, Wingate was to get six brigades largely from the reorganization of the British 70th Division, coupled with a brigade from the 81st West African Division.

Wingate's expanded attack strategy was novel but realistic. Air power would revolutionize LRP, as fighter-bombers became aerial artillery

and the transports and gliders provided supplies, armaments, reinforcements and casualty evacuation with precision, enabled by state-of-the-art radio communications. The need for sea- or land-borne lines of communication for an invading force was over. Unlike Operation *Longcloth*, Wingate envisioned Special Force being able to stay and fight at locales of choice (i.e. at the 'strongholds'), rather than dispersing or having to fight their way back through an enclosing enemy. The Chindit leader now coupled his tactical concept of movement with proximate defended garrisons.

Wingate addresses a contingent of Col. Philip Cochran's USAAF No. 1 Commando (behind Wingate's left shoulder) about details for the upcoming Operation *Thursday* in 1944. (IWM, MH 7877)

Wingate was modernizing warfare by shaping his visions into realities in the remote and desolate Burmese theatre. The absence of roads, tremendous distances, and a formidable terrain made operations almost non-sustainable, as the Japanese soon learnt in their *U-Go* offensive in Assam in 1944.

His new USAAF allies were colonels Philip Cochran and John Alison. In a meeting with Wingate, Cochran assured Wingate that 'the Chindits had only to "dream up" ideas and he would put them into operation. We will do anything you ask us to do, but it is up to you to produce the ideas for us to carry out'. So began the amazing collaboration that was to revolutionize Wingate's ideas of LRP, with the Cochran/Alison team providing the necessary air component to implement the emerging doctrine. To Cochran, 'with his radio direction, Wingate used his guerrilla columns in the same way that fighter-control HQ directs planes out on a mission. It was an adaptation of air to jungle, an application of radio-controlled air-war tactics to a walking war in the trees and the weeds.... When I left him, I was beginning to assimilate some of the flame of this guy Wingate'. To accomplish this feat, Cochran and Alison would have Mustang fighters, Mitchell bombers, Dakota and Commando transport aircraft, 100 light

1. 5 February 1944: 16th Brigade, under Brig. Fergusson, starts its march into Burma.
2. 6 March 1944: After Broadway air-landing field is secured, engineers arrived to create airstrips for Dakotas and light planes and convert it into a Wingate-styled 'stronghold'.
3. 6–7 March 1944: A second operation begins to fly by glider the advance guard of 111th Brigade into Chowringhee, a landing zone some 50 miles south-west of Broadway between the Shweli and Irrawaddy Rivers.
4. 111th Brigade marches north-west across the Irrawaddy to the vicinity of Banmauk to ultimately provide assistance for 16th Brigade once it arrived in the Indaw area (on 20 March) to set up a stronghold, Aberdeen, which it would garrison and patrol from for six weeks against the Japanese at Indaw.
5. From Chowringhee, Morrisforce and Dahforce start their north-eastward trek to assist Stilwell on a line Bhamo–Myitkyina.
6. 16–17 March 1944: Calvert takes five columns of 77th Brigade from Broadway and clashes with IJA forces at Henu. The Chindits

secure the area and began to fortify what is to become the White City stronghold.
7. 1 April 1944: IJA 24th Independent Mixed Brigade (IMB), reinforced to division size, establishes its base in the Sepein–Mawlu area and launches a full-scale attack on White City on 6 April.
8. Early May 1944: 111th Brigade established a new stronghold, Blackpool, in the Mogaung area and immediately is attacked before a strong defensive perimeter can be constructed.
9. 9–10 May 1944: White City evacuated as the theatre of Chindit operations shifts north to assist Stilwell's offensive towards Myitkyina and Mogaung. Broadway and Aberdeen are also abandoned.
10. 25 May 1944: remnants of the 111th Brigade evacuated from Blackpool under intense IJA attacks.
11. 6 June 1944: 77th Brigade launches its attack on Mogaung and captures it three weeks later.
12. 27 August 1944: The last Chindits are evacuated to India.

Wingate's area of operations in Burma during Operation *Thursday*, March 1944

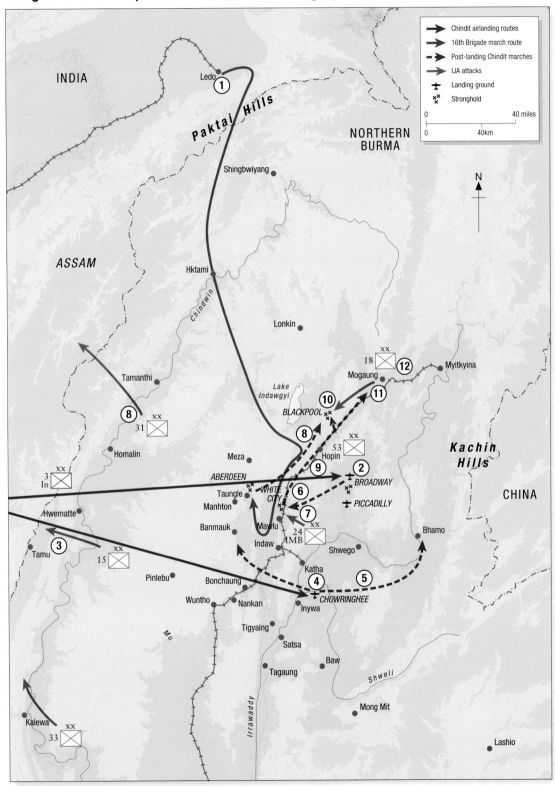

Waco gliders lined up at an airfield in India in March 1944 for airlifting Wingate's initial Chindit brigades into Burma for Operation *Thursday*. (IWM, EA 21408)

aircraft for evacuation and reconnaissance, and over 200 Waco gliders, along with RAF Vengeance dive bombers for close air support.

In December 1943, after Wingate had recovered from a near-lethal bout of typhoid fever (probably acquired from rashly drinking contaminated water from an empty flower vase on his return to India from England), Special Force's organization for Operation *Thursday* was complete. Calvert commanded 77th Indian Brigade (composed of elements of the King's Regiment, the Lancashire Fusiliers, the South Staffords and the 4th and 9th Gurkha Rifles). Lentaigne led the 111th Indian Brigade, with the King's Own Royal Regt. and a battalion of Cameronians as its core. Bernard Fergusson commanded the 16th Brigade, which was composed of elements of the Queen's Royal Regt., 2nd Bn. Leicestershire Regt., and elements of the Royal Artillery and Royal Armoured Corps. The 14th and 23rd Brigades were composed of men from the former British 70th Division. The sixth and final brigade was the 3rd West African Brigade, which arrived in India in November 1943. Special Force numbered 23,000 men. Major-General G. W. Symes, commander of the disbanded 70th Division, became Wingate's deputy. Lieutenant-General William Slim, who had also been in Ethiopia under Platt, was to command the Fourteenth Army as of 15 October 1943, with Wingate serving under him. For security reasons, Special Force had also received a new name, 3rd Indian Division. To complete the chain of command, Mountbatten as Commander-in-Chief, South East Asia Command (SEAC), had Gen. Sir George Giffard, in charge of 11th Army Group, as his land force commander. Lieutenant-General Joseph W. Stilwell was deputy to Mountbatten but also reported to Generalissimo Chiang Kai-Shek.

A heavily laden Dakota transport of the RAF about to parachute supplies to Chindits in the Burmese jungle below. (IWM, IND 5277)

The new aspect to Wingate's LRP doctrine was to establish defended areas wherever his brigades were operating. Their entry into Burma would be made by aircraft and gliders. This initial group of roughly two columns would occupy a field that would be converted into a landing strip for larger transport aircraft. Then, the transport aircraft would bring in the rest of the brigade. Wingate envisioned that these defended areas or 'strongholds' would be operational within 36 hours and ready to disrupt Japanese installations and communications in the vicinity. This idea of 'stronghold' originated from Wingate's abandoned plan to establish one in March 1943 in the forests of Bambwe Taung. The notion was that such a defended locale would enable columns to retire into it for safety and then set out on raids from its perimeter. With supply and relief, these strongholds could become virtual offensives on their own. Although there was a brief disagreement over which troops should garrison Wingate's strongholds, Slim did offer to furnish the Chindit garrisons with a number of 25-pdr field and Bofors 40mm AA guns. Slim also offered the 3rd/9th Gurkha Rifles of 26th Division as a 'force that might with advantage be flown in to take over from the LRP forces'. On 20 February 1944, Wingate was to document his idea of the stronghold, which was taken from the book of Zechariah: 'Turn ye to the Stronghold, ye prisoners of hope'. Wingate added, 'The motto of the Stronghold is "No Surrender"'.

Wingate (second from right) studies unexpected aerial reconnaissance photos with, (left to right) Colonels Cochran, Alison, and Scott; Air Marshal Baldwin, Brigadiers Calvert and Tulloch (to the right of Wingate) at Lalaghat airfield. After noting teak logs at Piccadilly, a designated glider landing field, Wingate and Calvert decided to shift 77th Indian Brigade's landing to Broadway. Wingate's behaviour at this impromptu meeting has been disputed and has led to controversy. (IWM, MH 7884)

As early as 16 January 1944, Wingate provided evidence to Mountbatten that a Japanese move up to the Chindwin River was the preparatory stage for an offensive against Assam. His believed that the Japanese would be compelled to use the 'long bad vulnerable roads of Burma' and that this offensive would be 'strong and damaging and that before it was overcome 11th Army Group might have to face the temporary loss of all Manipur'. This prediction was quite accurate as later events showed. On 14–15 March, the Japanese invaded Assam in three-division strength from the north of Homalin and from the centre of their Chindwin front, in Operation *U-Go*.

In January 1944, Wingate formulated his plan. 77th Indian Brigade was to fly into the Kaukkwe Valley north-east of Katha to establish a stronghold and disrupt the railway from Indaw to Myitkyina, as well as block the Bhamo–Lashio road. Lentaigne's 111th Indian Brigade would also fly into the area south of Pinlebu and form a stronghold to attack Japanese communications around Wuntho and in the Mu Valley. Fergusson's 16th Brigade, which was the first to depart by overland march from Ledo on 5 February, would head south to establish a stronghold north of Indaw to attack the Bonchaung Gorge, the Meza Bridge and, ultimately, capture the Indaw airfield. Two smaller forces were organized: one detached from 111th Indian Brigade, consisting of the 4th/9th Gurkha Rifles ('Morrisforce'), under Lt. Col. J. R. Morris, the other a detachment of Burma Rifles under Lt. Col. D. C. Herring, known as 'Dahforce'. These smaller detachments would operate on Japanese positions along the Bhamo–Myitkyina road and in the

A Waco glider landing amid flying debris from another crashed glider at Broadway. (IWM, SE 7039)

Chindits and US Army engineers sit around a wrecked glider at Broadway. With limited supplies and equipment, these men managed to transform a furrowed airfield littered with wreckage into a serviceable one. (IWM, EA 20827)

Kachin Hill country to the east of it. The second wave of the Chindit force would be the 14th and 23rd Brigades, along with the 3rd West African Brigade for garrison duty, which would be held in reserve for relief or exploitation. Slim, Giffard and the air commanders would have final approval to commit the garrison battalions or the reserve brigades. Wingate's orders for Operation *Thursday* were issued on 4 February by Gen. Slim and Maj. Gen. Stratemayer, USAAF Commander Far East. He was instructed to help the advance of Stilwell's force from Ledo; to create a favourable situation for the Chinese to advance from the Yunnan across the Salween River; to inflict maximum confusion, damage and loss on the enemy forces in north Burma.

To reach the Chindwin River, Fergusson's 16th Brigade climbed over and down the Paktai Hills and crossed the river unchallenged on 28 February north-east of Hkamti courtesy of a decoy crossing south of the town. Fergusson's boats and engines for the Chindwin crossing had been landed by glider near the river, while the decoy party was flown in by light aircraft. The airfields for the departures of 77th and 111th Indian Brigades were Hailakandi and Lalaghat, 70 miles from Imphal, and Tulihal, much closer to the base. Air landing zones in the Kaukkwe Valley were called 'Broadway' to the north and 'Piccadilly', about 35 miles south of the former. Glider-borne infantry would leave Lalaghat along with US Army engineers with jeeps, bulldozers and graders to create the Dakota transport airfields for subsequent *matériel* and personnel reinforcement. Two further air landing zones were 'Chowringhee', between the Irrawaddy and Shweli rivers, for Morrisforce; and 'Templecombe' for Dahforce, about 35 miles due south of Myitkyina.

On 5 March Calvert's 77th Indian Brigade was to take off by towed gliders from Lalaghat. In the late afternoon, one of Cochran's aerial reconnaissance planes obtained photographs of the Kaukkwe Valley. Wingate had forbidden such flights over the operational area, but Cochran had nonetheless arranged it. The photographs showed that teak logs covered all of Piccadilly's level space. Wingate, Calvert, Tulloch, Scott, Cochran, Alison and Air Marshal Baldwin all knew that glider landing there was now impossible and the entourage wondered if security for the operation had been breached. Wingate conferred with Slim for 20 minutes and then left the decision as to whether to continue the operation to Calvert, who enthusiastically agreed to go. The 77th Indian Brigade's commander wanted to take his entire force into Broadway and have a slower build-up rather than splitting his command to land at Broadway and across the Irrawaddy at Chowringhee, which was also 111th Brigade's air-landing site.

Cochran re-directed his pilots to 'a better place to go' and after a delay of just over an hour, 61 of an originally planned 80 gliders were towed by the Dakotas. In addition to 14 gliders that broke away from their Dakotas in full flight, Calvert's remaining gliders initially crashed badly on reaching the ground causing him to send a coded phrase ('Soya Link') to Wingate that conveyed erroneously that the Japanese had laid an ambush. Wingate's entourage was despondent and plans were hastily formed to evacuate those that landed at Broadway, while others still on their way were ordered back. However, by dawn, the more favourable code ('Pork Sausage') was received that there was no Japanese ambush. Out of Calvert's 542 men that landed by glider, 24 had been killed and 30 badly wounded. Despite the glider wreckage, a bulldozer was salvaged to begin the hasty construction of a Dakota airstrip, which Calvert told Wingate could begin receiving by that evening. The gliders that had crash-landed in either western Burma or Assam, created an unplanned diversion and diverted Japanese attention away from the landing zones.

A bulldozer driven by a US Army engineer creates a runway for aircraft at Broadway within hours of the almost disastrous glider landings the night before. (IWM, SE 7932)

On the night of 6 March an additional 900 men were flown into Broadway and Calvert's initial build-up was complete by the morning of 10 March. The initial party of 111th Indian Brigade flew into Chowringhee in 14 gliders during the night of 7 March. The following night, Lentaigne's remaining force arrived in Dakotas. Lentaigne was to take his brigade west of the Irrawaddy and establish a stronghold five miles south of Banmauk. From Chowringhee, Morrisforce and Dahforce were to start their separate missions. Shortly after the Chindits left Chowringhee, the Japanese bombed the landing field.

After supervising the construction of Broadway as a stronghold, Calvert led out five Chindit columns to the west of the railway to create a smaller stronghold to serve as a communications post from the south to Myitkyina. He captured the railway town of Henu by bayonet charge and fierce hand-to-hand combat at a mile or so to the north of the Mawlu rail station. This stronghold was eventually called 'White City' because of all the parachutes festooning the trees. Thanks to the establishment of White City, Japanese troop and supply movement on the railway from Katha and Indaw to Myitkyina was interrupted.

Chindits manually fill in furrows from dragged teak logs to hasten construction of the airfield at Broadway on 6 March 1944. A wrecked Waco glider is seen in the left background. (IWM, SE 7956)

On 11 March, Wingate issued an Order of the Day to his 3rd Indian Division: 'Our first task is fulfilled. We have inflicted a complete surprise on the enemy. All our columns are inserted in the enemy's guts. The time has come to reap the fruit of the advantage we have gained…. This is a moment to live in history. It is an enterprise in

Chindits work beside a bulldozer and scraper to fill in furrows at the Broadway airfield. (IWM, EA 20828)

which every man who takes part may feel proud one day to say I WAS THERE'. On 20 March Wingate flew into White City for an inspection tour with Calvert and gave some very helpful suggestions. He then flew on to a landing ground prepared by Fergusson's 16th Brigade at Taungle in the Meza Valley. In this valley, between Taungle and Manhton, where the Meza and Kalat rivers converge, Fergusson decided to situate the 'Aberdeen' stronghold. Here, Wingate and Fergusson discussed the assault on Indaw by 16th Brigade. Wingate wanted Fergusson to start the attack immediately so he could bring in the reserve 14th and 24th Brigades by Dakota. He wanted to pre-empt Fourteenth Army from using them as regular infantry in the defence against Operation *U-Go* in Assam. However, on 21 March Slim needed to relieve IV Corps in Assam, so he and Wingate agreed to fly in 14th Brigade, along with the garrison troops of 3rd West African Brigade, to Aberdeen immediately. On 22 March gliders containing American engineers and their equipment landed at Taungle to enlarge the Aberdeen strip into a Broadway-type airfield complex. The first section of 14th Brigade landed at Taungle on 23 March just around the same time that Fergusson and elements of 16th Brigade had left the stronghold for his attack on Indaw. From there, these reinforcements were to move to a place some 15 miles west of Wuntho and 60 miles south-west of Aberdeen in order to disrupt the communications from Wuntho and Indaw to the Chindwin, thereby drawing off some pressure on IV Corps west of the river.

On the morning of 24 March Wingate returned, by air, to Broadway. From there, he went to White City by light aircraft to view the renewed IJA assault

Unloading gliders for airstrip construction following the landings at Broadway during Operation *Thursday*, March 1944

The initial glider landings at Broadway occurred during the night of 5–6 March, but only seven of the American engineers and one of their officers had survived, along with only one bulldozer and a jeep with towable scraper for construction equipment. A number of deep furrows across Broadway destroyed the leading gliders' undercarriages and these Wacos could not be moved from the path of other gliders landing. Soon the area was strewn with wreckage. Calvert's Chindits immediately used shovels to fill in the furrows (1), while a bulldozer/scraper (2) in the distance smoothed Broadway's airfield perimeter to accept more gliders and ultimately Dakota transports to reinforce their stronghold. Other Chindits unloaded newly-arrived Waco gliders, which carried a Bofors 40mm anti-aircraft gun of the 267/69 Troop Light AA Regt. (3) for Broadway's defence, and a multi-purpose jeep (4). In the foreground Wingate (5) confers with Lt. Walter Scott (6).

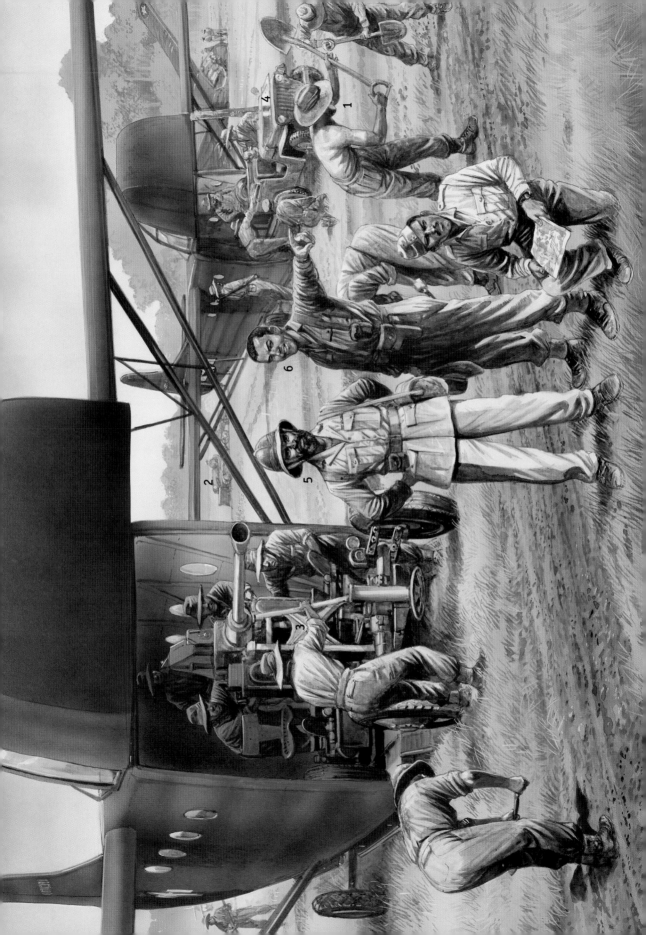

Chindits stand along the airstrip at Broadway soon after its completion. An American L5 liaison aircraft used for casualty evacuation is seen on the runway. (IWM, SE 7937)

against this stronghold. Wingate flew on to Aberdeen to inspect the progress with the airfield there and the arrival of 14th Brigade He returned to Broadway to board the Mitchell bomber for his return to Imphal. After a meeting with Air Marshal Baldwin at Imphal, Wingate decided to use the Mitchell bomber again to visit Cochran's No. 1 Air Commando at Lalaghat. Somewhere between the Bishenpur Hills and Lalaghat, Wingate's aircraft crashed and everyone, including several USAAF officers and NCOs, were killed. The wreckage was spotted by aerial reconnaissance on 25 March, and by 29 March, a foot patrol from Chindit HQ found the destroyed aircraft. Although identification was very difficult after the fire, Wingate's Wolseley-style solar topee was found. Wingate's friend, Brig. Derek Tulloch declined the offer to assume command of 3rd Indian Division and instead recommended Brig. Lentaigne of 111th Indian Brigade.

Although 16th Brigade had initially failed to take Indaw, a renewed assault succeeded on 27 April. It turned out that the airfield at Indaw was only a fair-weather one, so 16th Brigade was evacuated by air by the beginning of May and Aberdeen was abandoned. A few days later, Broadway and White City were also abandoned. These strongholds could not hold out during the monsoon rains because the airstrips there could not be converted to all-weather fields. After this, the 77th Indian, 14th and 111th Indian Brigades operated on Stilwell's front to Myitkyina. 23rd Brigade never deployed for LRP use, although it fought well with Slim and his Fourteenth Army. Another stronghold, called Blackpool, was established west of Mogaung, which was on the railway to Myitkyina. Calvert's capture of Mogaung, which was the last major Chindit operation, was successfully completed on 27 June.

OPPOSING COMMANDERS

The Grand Mufti of Jerusalem and the Arab Revolt

The Arab Revolt occurred in Palestine amid waves of violence from 1936 to 1939. The Higher Arab Committee (HAC), a collection of well-to-do anti-imperial Arabs organized the first of two distinct phases. Although their ultimate aim was civil unrest, strikes and other forms of protest were the main tactics utilized. By October 1936, the British administrators in Palestine had ended the internal strife by implementing political concessions and appealing to other Arab rulers in Saudi Arabia, Transjordan, Iraq and Yemen to urge, via diplomatic channels, for an end to the unrest. Finally, with two British divisions deployed to Palestine, the threat of martial law also greatly contributed to ending this first wave of insurrection.

The second wave of violence broke out during the latter part of 1937 and it increasingly targeted British administrators and troops, as well as Jews in urban areas and within settlements. Soon after Wavell arrived in Palestine in 1937 Arab terrorists in Nazareth murdered Lewis Andrews, the District Commissioner for Galilee, on 26 September 1937. Wavell cracked down hard on the HAC, and several Arab leaders were deported to the Seychelles, off the east coast of Africa in the Indian Ocean. However, the violence against British authority in Palestine still raged on. Not only was the Iraq Petroleum Company's pipeline to Haifa regularly set ablaze, but telephone lines and passenger railways were also sabotaged. Attacks against Jews and, even moderate Arabs who worked for the British administration were commonplace. Fomenting much of this insurrection was the Grand Mufti of Jerusalem, Haji Amin el Husseini, along with an Arab terrorist in Syria, Fawzi el-Qawujki. El-Qawujki was a soldier in France's Syrian Army during the decade preceding the Arab Revolt, who had received military training at France's premier military academy, Saint-Cyr. He was known for his ferocity towards prisoners and after World War II erupted, he fought Britain on the side of Vichy France, who pardoned him in 1941. Both the Grand Mufti and El-Qawujki enjoyed the support of Arab governments outside Palestine and Syria.

Wingate (centre) with his trademark sun helmet and rifle, at Broadway awaiting a night supply drop. Left to right, Colonels Merrill and Alison, Brig. Calvert, Capt. Borrow (Wingate's ADC), Col. Scott and Maj. Francis are with him. (IWM, MH 7873)

Haji Amin el Husseini, the Grand Mufti of Jerusalem, was chief of the extremists, the leader of the religious community, and organized the policy of Arab terrorism against British and Jewish targets. The Mufti had also encouraged Syrian terrorists to undermine King Abdullah I's government in Transjordan with the specific intent of unifying territory on both sides of the river Jordan in the Arab cause. After the British response to the insurgency, Husseini hid inside the temple in the centre of the Old City. With the British forbidden to arrest him in the temple area, the Mufti believed himself safe in a sanctuary, and continued to wage his subversive mission against the British and Jews. In mid-October 1937, the Mufti escaped from Jerusalem and was stopped by the French authorities off the coast of Lebanon. The French refused to extradite him and he escaped from Lebanon to Iraq before joining the Nazis in Berlin – on the ancient principle that 'my enemy's enemy is my friend'. With the Mufti under their patronage the Germans now gave open encouragement to the Arab insurrection. Rumours circulated that the Nazis were paying Husseini £10,000 a year to ignite the violence in Palestine. Although, the Mufti orchestrated much of the Arab terrorism against both the British and Jews in Palestine, his anti-imperial struggle always had international dimensions. He left behind him in Jerusalem an Arabic translation of an Irish Republican Army (IRA) handbook about fighting the British. The Grand Mufti made his way to Baghdad at the end of the Arab Revolt in 1939, where Iraqi officials conspiring against the British, gave him sanctuary along with other modes of support. After the Iraqi rebellion ended in 1941, Haji Amin el-Husseini again travelled to Germany. Demonstrating his zeal for an international approach for Muslim rebellion, the Grand Mufti was instrumental in attracting Bosnian Muslims into Himmler's SS, where they sowed havoc in the Balkans during World War II.

Amedeo di Savoia, Duke of Aosta

The Duke of Aosta was a cousin of King Victor Emmanuel III of Italy and was appointed Governor-General and Viceroy of Italian East Africa in November 1937. Born in 1898, his military service included becoming both a fighter pilot and air force general. He was a chivalrous, cultured Anglophile who had been educated in England, and was greatly admired and respected by those who served under him. For these reasons, among others, he was not well liked by Mussolini, although the duke's positive governance had reduced the strength of Ethiopian resistance after Emperor Haile Selassie's abdication, everywhere except the Gojjam Province. As viceroy, he had exhibited a greater degree of reconciliation with the native population than his more bellicose and bigoted predecessor, General Graziani, who ruled with a reign of terror. The duke was chosen to replace Graziani in Italian East Africa when Graziani's barbaric practices damaged relations with the local inhabitants. Prior to the outbreak of war in June 1940, the duke's policies also had improved border relations with the British administration in both the Sudan and Kenya.

However, Mussolini believed that the Duke of Aosta lacked ruthlessness and commanding military ability. The duke was a pragmatist, who realized that, despite his numerical superiority in Italian East Africa, his geographical isolation would almost certainly nullify any meaningful resupply and reinforcement, and ultimately this would lead to defeat. The situation of Italian Somaliland, Eritrea and Ethiopia was strategically weak because the sea communications could easily be cut, and even the air communications were liable to be interrupted by an enemy based in the Middle East. The duke commanded a force of 340,000, the vast majority being Italian-officered *ascari* or local levies, with the remainder being Italian Blackshirts, carabinieri, or grenadiers. In contrast, the British under both Platt and Cunningham had fewer troops but were able to reinforce their forces from Egypt, India and South Africa, whereas the Italian LOC were always stretched and vulnerable to attack. For his advance into Italian Somaliland and Ethiopia, Cunningham was able to use the East African ports both on the Indian Ocean and eventually on the Red Sea.

The Duke of Aosta was so uneasy about the state of his forces that in April 1940, he went to Rome to review his concerns with Mussolini and his army leaders. The duke wanted to assume the

Wingate being briefed by his brigadier and long-time friend, Derek Tulloch (left) after Operation *Thursday* had commenced. (IWM, MH 7867)

offensive as soon as war was declared in June 1940 and advance into the Sudan before substantial British reinforcements arrived. However sensible this seemed, Marshal Badoglio, the Minister of Defence in Rome, overruled him, and insisted that the duke's troop dispositions were to be strictly defensive. Although Mussolini and his advisors ordered the duke to remain on the defensive, they also prohibited his retreat into the Ethiopian Highland interior, forcing him to hold out for as long as possible. This conflicting set of orders ultimately confined the duke's overwhelming numerical force to limited attacks on British garrisons on the Sudan frontier, such as at Gallabat, Kassala and Kurmuk in July 1940 and on Moyale on the Kenyan border.

Wavell's strategy was that once the Italian threat to Egypt was removed by his resounding victory during Operation *Compass* from December 1940 to February 1941, he would turn his attention to eliminating the Italian army in East Africa. Wavell outlined these plans to Platt and Cunningham in Cairo in early December 1940, just days before the start of Operation *Compass*.

After Cunningham had begun his attack on Addis Ababa in early April 1941, Aosta took his garrison north to Alma Alagi, which he believed to be near-impregnable, with mountain peaks in excess of 11,000ft high fortified with trench works. At Alma Alagi, Aosta was once again besieged by a pincer movement, with Cunningham's troops moving north from the Ethiopian capital and the 5th Indian Division driving southwards from Asmara in Eritrea. The main attack by the 5th Indian Division began on 4 May, followed by the arrival of Cunningham's troops on 10 May to complete the encirclement of the duke's final redoubt. He surrendered to Cunningham with remnants of his army on 19 May 1941, in part to prevent a massacre of the wounded. Always chivalrous, the duke agreed to surrender unconditionally, provided that Cunningham accorded his Italian troops the 'honours of war', in which they would be permitted to march past a reviewing stand and give and receive a salute before laying down their arms. On 19 May, the duke with about 5,000 of his soldiers did, indeed, march past a British guard of honour and then surrendered their arms, a throwback to the 18th century's fields of battle. From a strategic point of view, the victory of Platt, Cunningham, and Wingate over the Italians enabled Wavell to realize one of his paramount goals, namely, to open the Red Sea to American and British shipping and dramatically shorten the naval lines of communications to India and the Far East. The Duke of Aosta died in captivity in 1942 in Kenya.

Japanese commanders

On 27 March 1943, Burma Area Army HQ was set up under the command of Lieutenant-General M. Kawabe to control 15th Army and 55th Division, which were allotted to the defence of central and northern Burma and Arakan, respectively. Kawabe's primary task was Burma's defence, but he also had the charge of planning Japanese offensive operations across the Chindwin frontier into Assam. Lieutenant-General Renya Mutaguchi initially commanded the formidable IJA 18th Division, as part of the 15th Army, in northern Burma. He was described as a 'heavy-bodied, bullet-headed officer

Troops of the West African Brigade board a Dakota transport to reinforce Broadway. Not only did this new modality for Operation *Thursday* enable Wingate to fight larger IJA units but it also allowed him to pioneer his concept of a defended 'stronghold'. (IWM, IND 7046)

with hard eyes and thick lips who fiercely overrode the intractable problem of supply and whose wrath was so feared by his staff that they did not press their doubts.'

Earlier in his career, Mutaguchi was present at the Japanese capture of Peking in 1937, and Kawabe was Chief of Staff Expeditionary Force in China. At the outbreak of the China Incident in 1937, both Kawabe and Mutaguchi were serving in north China, the former as a brigade commander, and the latter as a regimental commander. When not demonstrating his extreme condescension towards his seemingly inept Chinese opponents, Mutaguchi ridiculed his other vanquished enemy, the British, who he swiftly defeated at Singapore with the IJA 18th Division.

In Burma, Mutaguchi operated from his divisional HQ in Maymyo in the very buildings where Stilwell had met Alexander, Wavell, and Wingate at the start of the retreat in 1942. As commander of the 18th Division, Mutaguchi was involved in the operations to defend northern Burma against the Chindit assault in Operation *Longcloth*. Upon being promoted to lead the IJA 15th Army in March 1943, Mutaguchi had under his command 18th Division led by General Shinichi Tanaka, which faced the Chindits and Stilwell in the north; 56th Division facing Chiang Kai-Shek's Yoke Force in the east; and the 33rd Division facing the British on the Chindwin. Tanaka was also among the vanquishers at Singapore, Malaya, and Burma. The 15th Army was reinforced by the 31st Division, commanded by Lieutenant-General Kotuku Sato, which had some units in both China and the Pacific. Elements of this division began to arrive in Burma in June 1943 and this build-up was completed by September. It was Lt. Gen. Sato who hurled the 31st Division against the British garrison at Kohima in India during the *U-Go* offensive.

The British senior commanders in Delhi may have been derisive and willing to ignore any important outcome of Wingate's first Chindit expedition in March 1943 (Operation *Longcloth*), but Mutaguchi later conceded that it had changed his entire strategic thinking. Mutaguchi had scrutinized Wingate's tactics and his use of the Burmese terrain and concluded, as Wingate demonstrated, that troops would be mobile with pack transport in northern and western Burma only during the dry season. Wingate had also shown that it was possible for units to attack across the main north–south grain of the rivers and mountains of Burma. The Japanese general's own revelation, along with intelligence of the British build-up at Imphal, convinced Mutaguchi that he must eventually attack Imphal and Kohima to pre-empt another British offensive to be launched from India in 1944. He also realized the improving capabilities and battle efficiency of the British-Indian troops. These were not the same retreating, defeated Commonwealth troops of 1941–42. However, prior to that invasion, Mutaguchi argued that the 15th Army line of defence should be moved westward, to at least the Chindwin River, or even possibly to the hills on the Assam–Burma border.

On 11 April 1944, Mutaguchi was relieved of the responsibility of looking after northern Burma and was given the single task of the Imphal/Kohima offensive. His superior, Kawabe, had concluded that the best course would be to attack the British before they had time to complete their preparations for an offensive, capture their base at Imphal and prevent them launching any offensive into Burma. An advance into central Assam was beyond the capabilities

A Chindit casualty is lifted into an L5 light aircraft for evacuation to Assam. Casualty evacuation was new for Operation *Thursday* and certainly improved morale as well as survival rates for the injured. (IWM, SE 7947)

of the army as it then was. Having witnessed the Chindit operation of 1943, the Japanese for their part had come to the conclusion that they would be unable to defeat the threatened Allied offensive by remaining defensive-minded, and that an invasion of Assam in order to capture the Allied base at Imphal was their best course of action. The end of the summer of 1943 found the IJA planning an offensive for the dry season of early 1944.

Mutaguchi planned a three-division attack into India: 33rd Division under Gen. Yanagida to advance towards Imphal from the south against 17th Indian Division, which had fought in the retreat from Burma but was now substantially retrained and re-equipped; 15th Division under Gen. Yamauchi, together with units of the Indian National Army recruited from Indian prisoners of war, to attack Imphal in two prongs from the east; and, most significantly, 31st Division under Gen. Sato, which was to advance to Dimapur, the huge supply base, 11 miles long and a mile wide, which provided for the whole of Slim's Fourteenth Army. Mutaguchi intended that as soon as Kohima and Dimapur were captured, his victorious forces, accompanied by the Indian National Army and its leader, Subhas Chandra Bose, would advance into Bengal where the subjugated Indian populace would mount an internal insurrection against British rule and support his triumphant 'March on Delhi'.

It is seldom mentioned that Mutaguchi almost accomplished his strategic aim. If Mutaguchi's *U-Go* campaign of March–June 1944 had succeeded, British and American forces operating in Burma would have lost all contact with the west. An incorrect logistic and supply decision by this otherwise outstanding Japanese commander, along with the selfless bravery of Indian and British troops, thwarted his *U-Go* plan. His idea of beginning his offensive with only one month's rations and supplies, in anticipation of capturing the stores at Dimapur, became a significant factor in their ultimate defeat. The Japanese had no equivalent to the American and British air supply capabilities for troops on the ground in fortified positions (such as Wingate's strongholds) or on the move in the jungles and hills of Burma. Mountbatten, as Supreme Commander SEAC, had made the decision to transfer 30 supply aircraft from the 'Hump' operation to airlift 5th Indian Division back from the Arakan to bolster the defences of Kohima and

Dimapur and enable Slim's victory. There is little doubt that the airlift of 5th Indian Division played a vital role in the survival of Kohima and Dimapur, thereby depriving Mutaguchi of victory.

The Japanese generals' reaction to Operation *Thursday* was discordant as their own *U-Go* was underway. Mutaguchi initially believed that Wingate's second operation was too far into the northern Burmese interior to affect his own operations in Assam in the Kohima/Imphal area. However, his superior, Kawabe, took the Chindit assault seriously and cobbled together a force of about 20,000 troops to confront Wingate at Indaw in March/April 1944. Initially, this force was able to prevent Fergusson's assault on Indaw, but it was then diverted to attack Calvert at White City. With the failure of his forces on the Assam front, Mutaguchi sacked his three divisional generals in the course of Operation *U-Go* against Imphal and Kohima. After it failed, he was next to go and on 30 August 1944 was transferred to the General Staff in Tokyo. In a post-war letter to Colonel A. J. Barker, Mutaguchi wrote, 'On 26th March I heard on Delhi radio that General Wingate had been killed in an aeroplane crash. I realized what a loss this was to the British Army and said a prayer for the soul of this man in whom I had found my match'.

INSIDE THE MIND

In all of his endeavours – the Sudan, Palestine, Ethiopia and Burma – Wingate always exhibited personal bravery. In January 1941, upon escorting Selassie back into Ethiopia, a subordinate commented: 'the prospect of facing more than 30,000 Italians with only 50 British officers, 20 British non-commissioned officers, 800 Sudan Defence Force men, and 800 Ethiopian patriots did not concern Wingate in the slightest'. Wingate espoused, 'Given a population favourable to penetrate, a thousand resolute and well-armed men can paralyze for an indefinite period, the operations of 100,000'. This spirit compelled Wingate to name his Patriot troops in Ethiopia's Gojjam, Gideon Force, after the Bible's commander who defeated 15,000 Midianites with only 300 Hebrews.

Wingate's campaigns demonstrated traits of cunning and deception, coupled with a tendency towards the unorthodox. This was not too dissimilar from one of his patrons, Wavell, who had learned this craft from his mentor, Allenby. After all, it was Allenby whom Wingate lauded in his *Strategy in Three Campaigns* essay, citing his daring offensive in Palestine in 1917, in which deception, mobility, and skilful tactics all culminated in 'obtaining superiority at the decisive point', in order to overcome an opponent's numerical advantage. 'Bluff' was basically a propaganda tool and psychological attack that Wingate implemented during his Ethiopian campaign. Beginning at the key fortified town of Debra Markos on 30 March, Wingate communicated with the Italian commander, offering terms and implying that the Italians had a brief opportunity to surrender to

British regular forces, who would abide by the Geneva Convention, and if refusing this, they would be left to the Patriots, who would not.

A colleague of Wingate wrote, 'He rightly believed that the boldest methods are the safest. He could be ruthless too in getting what he wanted. He was determined to fulfil the task he was given by the President and Prime Minister at Quebec even if others were bent on obstructing him. His margins may have been thin (thick margins make every operation impossible) but he was not reckless.'

A subordinate, Lt. King-Clark, who served under Wingate in Palestine, noticed the 'sense of deliberate eccentricity, bordering on showmanship, which characterized his appearance… during this period… he began wearing the distinctive and old-fashioned Wolseley sun helmet which was to become his personal trademark in Ethiopia and Burma'. This was not too different from another great British commander, Bernard Law Montgomery, who possessed a flair for the eccentric, both in attire and language. Other aspects of Wingate's eccentricity included, scrubbing himself down stark-naked with a stiff hairbrush, consuming buffalo milk and devouring raw onions. According to the writer, Shelford Bidwell, Wingate was often like 'an Ancient Mariner in speech, holding his hapless interlocutor with piercing blue eyes and a numbing fund of recondite information, given to harangues, quarrelsome of personality and yet strangely persuasive, he was the perfect image of the unconventional and unorthodox soldier beloved of Wavell'.

Biographers focus more upon the impact of Wingate's personal psychology, as he suffered his first major attack of clinical depression during his SDF service, which probably arose from too much time spent in the monotonous Sudanese desert, his first sight of death and the sudden death of his sister. From a medical standpoint, critics regarded him as suffering from manic-depressive illness, while others thought that his erratic behaviour resulted from cerebral malaria. Wingate has been referred to as a 'cyclothyme', a manic-depressive passing from moods of profound despair in which he believed God had abandoned him, to euphoria, where he fulfilled his Lord's work. As Royle noted, 'When he was "up" he was fiercely inventive, displaying a passion and loquaciousness which dazzled those in his company. But when he was "down", the reverse was true and he was frequently left with the feeling that he was ahead of his time and that the rest of the world was out of step and somewhat mundane.'

Wingate's pronounced Zionist views, his service to Palestine and his close friendship with Jewish leaders may have belied a manic's hyper-religiosity, but his attachment to a Jewish homeland was part of his service to the underdog and a fondness for the Jewish race and their beliefs emanating from the pages of the Old Testament. To Smith and Bierman, 'The books of ancient Israel's kings and prophets were the General's unvarying guide in life, and often in battle, and he had assumed as his own the struggle of the modern Israelites to recover their ancestral homeland'. In Ethiopia, he, likewise, became an ardent supporter of Emperor Haile Selassie and the just restoration to his rule after ousting the Italians. Wingate's eccentricity may have been a cloak for his being 'a zealot in a conformist society like the army' and a man who did not take the middle road but straddled the extremist points of view.

Wingate almost destroyed his chances before his service in the Sudan had even got under way. Displaying all his impetuosity, he was often too loquacious and refused to accede to an interruption in his monologues. His fellow officers at Gedaref were often exposed to topics that were 'off limits' such as politics, especially Marxism, and religion. His egocentric focus and habit of airing his personal aspirations for the future often earned the ire of his fellow officers. Wingate was guilty of breaking a basic, though unwritten, army rule and it did not take long for his commanding officer, Lieutenant-Colonel Paddy Walsh, to warn him about his behaviour: 'You've been talking too much: a subaltern of your age should be seen and not heard, I don't like the things you say and I don't like you, but I will give you a choice. Either you shut up and keep your ideas about communism to yourself or I shall have you returned to your regiment with a black mark against you'.

Wavell wrote soon after Wingate's death, 'The truth is, I think, that he had in him such a consuming fire of earnestness for the work in hand that he could spare no effort to soothe or conciliate those with whom he worked. He thought deeply on other subjects than war, and I had occasional glimpses of a mind with stormy and interesting views on many matters, but there was never time to explore them before the warlike business in hand came uppermost again'.

In sum, the historian Andrew Roberts has posed the question whether Wingate 'was a genius and hero who single-mindedly pioneered a new form of jungle warfare that beat the Japanese at their own game, or whether he was an egomaniacal maverick whose two great Burmese expeditions of 1943 and 1944 cost more Allied lives than their meagre military returns were worth'.

WHEN WAR IS DONE

Wingate's campaigns and causes ended with his death in March 1944. However, a posthumous attack was levelled against Wingate in a vituperative account of the Chindit leader's contributions to the war in Burma. This appeared in 1961 in Maj. Gen. S. Woodburn Kirby's *The Official History of the War against Japan, Vol. III: The Decisive Battles*. Some have labelled this an 'exercise in literary envy against unorthodoxy and creativity'.

The animus between Wingate and Kirby went back to 1943, when the Chindit leader returned from Quebec and exhibited an aggressive and offensive stance in response to GHQ's near-total opposition to his plans for *matériel* and personnel requests for Operation *Thursday*. When Wingate flaunted his newly acquired access to Churchill, it humiliated Kirby, who was the Director of Staff Duties at GHQ, in front of his own staff. In a complaint to Mountbatten, Wingate 'rashly named Kirby as one of those who should be sacked for iniquitous and unpatriotic conduct'. Thus, Wingate became a particular enemy of Kirby, who in 1951 was appointed to write *The Official History of the War against Japan*. On those pages, Kirby took his revenge with a verbal offensive on Wingate's legacy. Kirby contemptuously wrote of Wingate:

> He was unwilling to co-operate with anyone not directly under his command and maintained an extraordinary degree of secrecy and furtiveness in his planning and in the conduct of his operations. He carried this to such an extent that one of his brigade commanders observed that he often seemed to forget the difference between what he planned and communicated to his staff and what he had merely thought of but not divulged.... He thus found himself facing problems which, by lack of experience, he was not equipped to solve. Always more determined on a course of action when he was opposed, he often rejected advice from those more experienced than himself, and so committed errors of judgment in tactical and technical matters as well as in planning.... In the field it is evident that he tended to react too easily to the enemy's movement and at times laid himself open to the charge of order, counterorder, disorder.... He had the fanaticism and drive to persuade others that they should be carried out, but he had neither the knowledge, stability nor balance to make a great commander. He never proved himself to be the man of genius whom the Prime Minister wished to appoint as Army Commander in charge of operations against the Japanese.... Instead of co-operating wholeheartedly with the army and air force commanders for the common good, he missed few opportunities of belittling them and questioning the value of orthodox force.... He disguised the conventional language of war by using such terms as 'stronghold' to denote a firm base or pivot of manoeuvre, issued orders of the day which spoke of columns being inserted into the enemy's guts and sent messages which compared the feat of a battalion in crossing the Chindwin to that of Hannibal crossing the Alps.

Kirby concluded his harangue: 'Although he served the Allied cause well by putting an almost forgotten army in the headlines and boosting morale, the very qualities which enabled him to win the support of the Prime Minister and the Chiefs of Staff and to create his private army in face of great difficulties reduced his value as a leader and a commander in the field'.

When Volume III of the *Official History* appeared in January 1961, The *Sunday Telegraph* asked, 'Will none of the eminent commanders of the last war who worked with Wingate, defend him against the outrageous conclusions of the Official History? Reading Maj. Gen. Kirby's edgy judgment it seems that the anti-Wingate party at the War Office was determined to have the last word'. To counter Kirby's malign treatment of Wingate's character and military reputation, a number of staunch defenders took to the pen. Bernard Fergusson, when he was about to become Governor-General of New Zealand, wrote to the *Scotsman* (14 February 1962) that 'the recent criticisms of Wingate cannot be allowed to stand'. David

Rooney wrote, 'When the Official History virtually says it was just as well an officer was killed, it cannot claim to be a fair or balanced assessment'. The mainstay of Wing Commander Sir Robert Thompson's memoirs, *Make for the Hills*, was a defence of Wingate, and clearly stated that Kirby's *Official History* 'originated mainly from Wingate's uncompromising and unsettling personality and the radicalism of his military ideas, which others in India simply did not understand.... It [Kirby's rant] was intended as a hatchet job by little men who could not have competed with him either in military argument or in battle.'

Even in death, Wingate was controversial. After the war, Wingate's wife wrote to Churchill that she wanted her husband's remains brought home. However, she was informed that the remains would be buried in the British war cemetery at Imphal in April 1947. A problem arose since the majority of the remains at the air crash were American, and it was suggested that they should be interred in a US war cemetery in the Philippines in 1949. Finally, on 10 November 1950, Wingate's remains were interred in the Arlington National Cemetery after it was agreed that 'the final resting place of intermingled remains in a common grave should be determined by the country whose dead were in the majority in that grave'. This prompted a storm of protest from the Wingate family that erupted into the British press and parliament.

Since the formal dedication of the gravesite at Arlington on 24 March 1974, 30 years after Wingate's death, every year Israel's ambassador to the United States lays a wreath in fond memory of 'the Friend'. The early leaders of Israel regarded him as the founder of their army and attributed their victory in the Six Day War of 1967 to his teaching. For this and his organization of the SNS, he has always been remembered as *Hayedid*, 'The Friend', in Israel.

A LIFE IN WORDS

Wingate's admirers describe him as 'brilliant and innovative' and believe that his Ethiopian campaign and operations in Burma played major roles in those Allied victories. His detractors believe that his military skills were exaggerated, while his campaigns were disastrous and irrelevant.

Field Marshal Slim's statements have been paradoxical as he initially praised Wingate for his genius immediately after his death: 'The number of men of our race in this war who are really irreplaceable can be counted on the fingers of one hand. Wingate is one of them. The force he built is his own; no one else could have produced it. He designed it, he raised it, he led it, inspired it and finally placed it where he was meant to place it – in the enemy vitals.' Yet, in his memoirs *Defeat into Victory*, published in 1956, Wingate received harsh criticism: 'With him, contact had too often been collision, for few could meet so stark a character without being violently attracted or repelled. To most he was either a prophet or an adventurer....

The trouble was, I think, that Wingate regarded *himself* as a prophet, and that always leads to a single-centredness that verges on fanaticism, with all its faults.' So Wingate, no longer a genius, had become 'strangely naïve when it came to the business of actually fighting the Japanese'. Operation *Longcloth* had been 'an expensive failure', that had given 'little tangible return for the losses it had suffered and the resources it had absorbed'. Perhaps Slim was negatively influenced by Kirby's ire towards Wingate as both were writing books on the Burma campaigns in the mid-1950s.

Louis Allen, in his treatise about Burma, wrote that Britain's Indian Army after the defeats of 1942, 'needed an immense uplifting of spirit. It needed Orde Wingate.... On the other hand the animus Wingate aroused in fellow commanders and distant staffs has also led to determined efforts to denigrate him and to reduce the impact of what he did.' Allen continued: 'devotees of the dull and staid will decry his [Wingate's] flamboyance, histrionic procedures, and the publicity which attended them. They miss the point. What the press and world opinion made of Wingate's initial exploits, infused a new spirit into the affairs of Burma; whatever the strategic upshot, whatever Wingate's psychological faults that renewal of spirit cannot be gainsaid.'

Robert Thompson, who served as air liaison on both Chindit operations, wrote in his memoirs, *Make for the Hills*, that Wingate was the first to realize that parachute and, later, air transport re-supply could augment the Chindit columns' mobility over the more numerous Japanese. Wingate alone among British Army and RAF senior staff advocated close air support, with Cochran's Air Commando's fighter-bombers providing the necessary 'artillery'. Thompson asserted that it was Wingate who advocated an overland offensive into Burma in 1943 even when the Japanese HQ believed it impossible. Finally, Thompson documented Operation *Thursday's* important contribution to the victory against the *U-Go* offensive in Assam and commented that when viewing the photographs of Slim and his Corps Commanders being knighted after Imphal, 'I see the ghost of Wingate present. He was unquestionably one of the great men of the century'.

In regard to Mutaguchi's view of the *U-Go* offensive, the IJA 15th Army commander wrote to one of Kirby's researchers that, 'Wingate's airborne tactics put a great obstacle in the way of our Imphal plan and were an important reason for its failure'. Mutaguchi, who had a reputation as a harsh judge of character and ability ranked Wingate's military concepts highly and admired his martial spirit.

Lieutenant-Colonel Terence Otway commanded 9th Bn. The Parachute Regiment in the Normandy landings on June 1944 and authored *Airborne Forces in World War II* in 1951. At odds with Kirby, Otway wrote that Operation *Longcloth* 'showed clearly the scope offered for applying new methods in the Burma theatre... proving that the power of supply and control was limited only by the number of aircraft and trained crews available'. During Operation *Thursday*, new concepts emerged, including casualty evacuation, close air support, airfield construction in hostile territory, and the stronghold concept. Otway argued that Operation

Thursday commenced with air landings of three Chindit brigades being 'embedded behind the lines and more or less at the centre of four Japanese divisions', which created a 'clamp' upon Japanese communications in northern Burma. For Otway, the Chindits of 1944 were much more than guerrilla forces since they contested strong Japanese units around their strongholds and inflicted heavy casualties. Otway concluded that Operation *Thursday's* main lesson was that 'Wingate's theories on Long Range Penetration… had proved correct in detail…. His force had gnawed a hole in the entrails of three Japanese divisions which weakened them to such an extent that their eventual collapse was complete.'

Bernard Fergusson, plucked by Wingate from the Joint Planning Staff at GHQ, wrote: 'Soon we had fallen under the spell of his almost hypnotic talk; and by and by we – some of us – had lost the power of distinguishing between the feasible and fantastic'. With his charm, Wingate could inspire those under his command, but was incapable of handling officialdom. He impressed Churchill and Roosevelt, but was viewed as insubordinate by Platt, Cunningham and Slim, among others. His unorthodox operations were brilliant, but his superiors believed he overreached in espousing that his methods could re-conquer all of Southeast Asia. However, on 24 July 1943, Churchill was intoxicated with Wingate's exuberant strategy and tactics as he wrote to General Ismay,

> See now how all these difficulties [in Burma] are mounting up, and what a vast expenditure of force is required for these trumpery gains. All the commanders on the spot seem to be competing with one another to magnify their demands and the obstacles they have to overcome… I consider Wingate should command the army against Burma. He is a man of genius and audacity, and has rightly been discerned by all eyes as a figure quite above the ordinary level. The expression "the Clive of Burma" has already gained currency. There is no doubt that in the welter of inefficiency and lassitude which has characterized our operations on the Indian front, this man, his force and his achievements stand out, and no mere question of seniority must obstruct the advance of real personalities to their proper stations in war.

SELECT BIBLIOGRAPHY

Allen, Louis, *Burma: The Longest War,* Phoenix Press: London, 2000
Anglim, Simon, *Orde Wingate and the British Army, 1922–1944,* Pickering & Chatto Publishers: London, 2010
Bidwell, Shelford, *The Chindit War: Stilwell, Wingate, and the Campaign in Burma: 1944,* MacMillan Publishing Co: New York, 1979
Bierman, John and Smith, Colin, *Fire in the Night: Wingate of Burma, Ethiopia, and Zion,* Random House: New York, 1999
Brayley, Martin and Ingram, Richard, *The World War II Tommy: British Army Uniforms,*

European Theatre 1939–45, The Crowood Press: Wiltshire, 1998

Calvert, Michael, *Fighting Mad,* The Adventurers Club: London, 1965

——, *Chindits: Long Range Penetration,* Ballantine Books: New York, 1973

——, *Prisoners of Hope,* Leo Cooper: London, 1996

Chinnery, Philip D, *March or Die,* Airlife Publishing Ltd: Shrewsbury, 1997

Churchill, Winston S, *World War II, Closing the Ring, vol. 5,* Houghton, Mifflin Company: Boston, 1951

Diamond, Jon, *Orde Wingate's Blurred Legacy,* WWII History, Sovereign Media: Herndon, 2008

——, *Archibald Wavell,* Osprey Publishing: Oxford, 2012

Fergusson, Bernard, *Beyond the Chindwin,* Pen & Sword: South Yorkshire: London, 1945

Gordon, John W, 'Wingate' in Keegan, John (Ed.), *Churchill's Generals,* Grove Weidenfeld: New York, 1991

Jeffreys, Alan, *The British Army in the Far East 1941–45,* Osprey Publishing: Oxford, 2005

——, *British Infantryman in the Far East 1941–45,* Osprey Publishing: Oxford, 2003

Kirby, S. W., *The War Against Japan, Vol. III: The Decisive Battles*, HMSO: London, 1961

Latimer, Jon, *Burma: The Forgotten War,* John Murray Publishing: London, 2004

Lyman, Robert, *Iraq 1941: The Battles for Basra, Habbaniya, Fallujah and Baghdad,* Osprey Publishing: Oxford, 2005

McLynn, Frank, *The Burma Campaign,* Yale Library of Military History: New Haven, 2011

Mead, Peter, *Orde Wingate and the Historians,* Merlin Books, Ltd: Devon, 1987

Mead, Richard, *Churchill's Lions, A Biographical Guide to the Key British Generals of World War II,* Spellmount: Gloucestershire, 2007

Moreman, Tim, *Chindit 1942–45,* Osprey Publishing: Oxford, 2009

Mosley, Leonard, *Gideon Goes to War,* Charles Scribner's Sons: New York, 1955

Otway, Terrence, *World War II 1939–1945, Army: Airborne Forces,* Imperial War Museum: London, 1990

Rolo, Charles J, *Wingate's Raiders: An Account of the Incredible Adventure That Raised the Curtain on the Battle for Burma,* George G. Harrap & Co, Ltd: London, 1944

Rooney, David, *Wingate and the Chindits,* Cassell & Co: London, 1994

Royle, Trevor, *Orde Wingate: A Man of Genius 1903–1944,* Frontline Books: London, 2010

Shirreff, David, *Bare Feet and Bandoliers: Wingate, Sandford, the Patriots and the Liberation of Ethiopia,* Pen & Sword: South Yorkshire, 1995

Slim, William, *Defeat Into Victory,* Papermac: London, 1956

Sumner, Ian, *British Commanders of World War II,* Osprey Publishing: Oxford, 2003

Sykes, Christopher, *Orde Wingate: A Biography,* The World Publishing Co: Cleveland, 1959

Thompson, Julian, *The Imperial War Museum Book of the War in Burma 1942-1945,* Pan Books: London, 2002

Thompson, Robert, *Make for the Hills*, Leo Cooper: Barnsley, 1989

Tulloch, Derek, *Wingate in Peace and War,* History Book Club, London, 1972

INDEX